MW01182264

010 Publishers, Rotterdam 2007

Alex de Voogt

Helidrome Architecture

Contents

5

Visible interest – welcoming the architect

6

Helidromes – a typology

Photo page 2-3: Crow's nest, Herbis Plaza Ent', Osaka, Japan

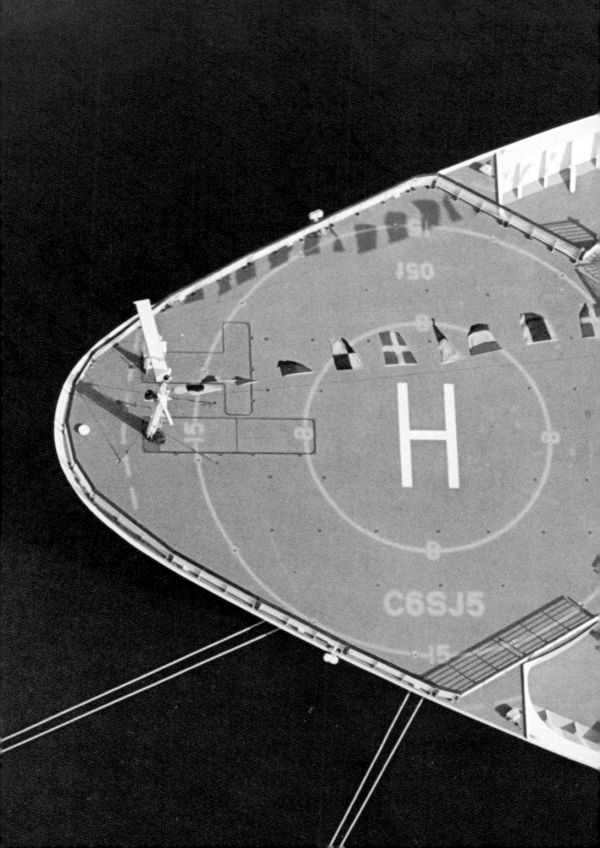

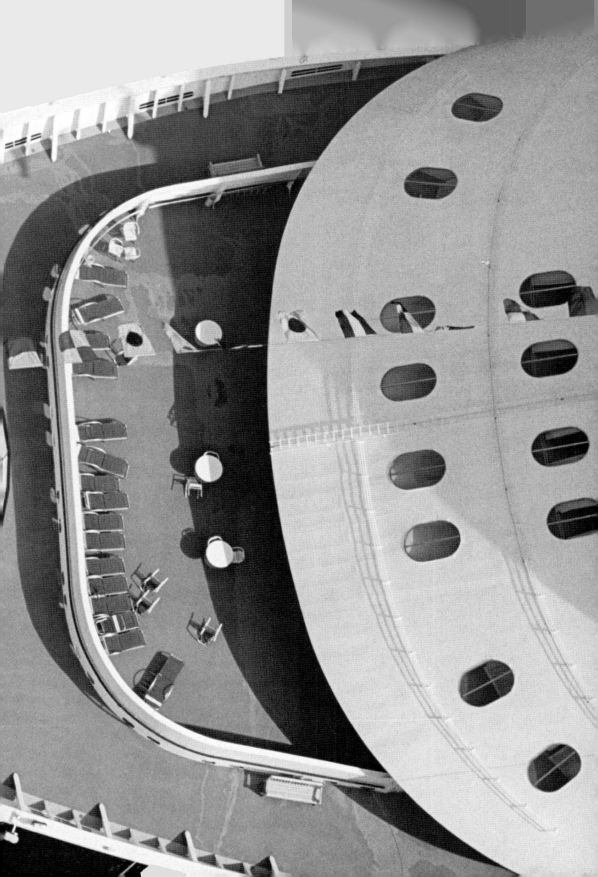

— Raising questions

The helidrome is a cleared space, an absence of obstacles or structures that could hinder the aircraft. It is designed so that the helicopter is free to fly safely. It ranges from a green pasture to a flat roof, and it seems characterized by the absence of architecture rather than its presence.

The exploration of the helidrome is central in this book. Its presence is constructed by placing it within the scenery, the country, the bureaucracy, and imagery of society and art. The material that constitutes its presence is fact and metaphor, list and anecdote. It dominates each chapter and is the main food for thought.

Helidrome Architecture presents an exploration and an analysis of built helidromes. It offers answers to the question of where helidromes are built, why they are built, and how they are built. These questions are answered with the collected data on large sets of helidromes and with discussions of individual helidrome designs.

The location of the helidrome

A helidrome is found on land or at sea, in one country or another, in the city or the countryside and in warm or cold climate zones. This geographical location of helidromes has taken this study around the world.

Even though the geographical location of a helidrome is sufficient for navigation, it is rarely the destination. Helidromes are at city centres, hospitals, police stations, offices, hotels, ships, or any other kind of structure. This type of location is an address rather than a set of co-ordinates on the map. The different kinds of buildings, according to their use, group helidromes in chapters or sections, often limited to one geographical zone.

At its address, the helidrome is placed on the ground or on a building, such as the roof. This height of the helidrome changes for each destination and geographical location, and is a necessary part of the discussion of helidrome architecture.

Helipads move from roof to roof, ground to roof and roof to ground on ever expanding hospitals. They lose licenses (Meander Hospital, Amersfoort), lose money (Metlife Building, New York) and access (Palace Hotel, Belo Horizonte), so that they disintegrate (Seculus Building, Belo Horizonte) or disappear (Refaja Hospital, Dordrecht). Even the ground-based helipad changes appearances often. The helipad is often less permanent than the building on which it rests.

The reasons for the helidrome

Countries and cities have laws and regulations that determine the possibilities for building a helidrome. Mountains, oceans, ice caps, and other remote locations provide reasons for the helidrome presence.

Not each building in a city or in a remote location is blessed with a helidrome. The function of the building hints at reasons of a different kind. Prestige, funds, safety, and other issues relating to the occupants or owners of the building become apparent. The helicopter itself also suggests reasons for the inviting helidrome, and such associations are detailed in a separate chapter on helicopters.

Helipad in decay, Seculus building,
Belo Horizonte, Brazil
← Helipad no longer in use, Refaja
Hospital, Dordrecht, The Netherlands

The presence of a helidrome on the building or on the ground requires a separate answer, since the reasons for building a helidrome may not be identical to the reasons for placing one on a roof.

The architecture of the helidrome
The architecture includes the location of, and reasons for, helidromes. It adds size, shape, and sometimes colour to the construction. The markings and safety netting are determined by government regulations. Accessories such as ramps, stairs and elevators mostly depend on the function of the building. The ground or the roof requires a mutually different support structure that determines the shape as it is seen from below.

A typology distinguishes formal types of helidromes, based on their distinguishing shapes. Each type of helidrome may be prevalent in a particular location, but it is the support structure that sets their architecture apart. It is the support structure of the helidrome that is visible from the ground and from the air, and it is the support structure that has creative input from an engineer or architect. It raises the flat helidrome to a distinguished level.

The locations, reasons, and shapes of helidromes are the ingredients of this study. They are not separate but integrated. Whereas the ingredients may be listed for each individual helidrome, the large sets of data cannot provide immediate answers to the questions raised. Instead of answering questions consecutively, an integrated approach is used.

The reasons and locations are related to the possibilities of the helicopter. A study of the role of helicopters in the arts presents both the image of the machine and its operations. It necessarily precedes a discussion of helidromes.

As with the controls that position a helicopter, the cross-coupling of locations, reasons, and shapes requires a continuous balancing act. The actors only settle down in the final chapter.

— Monuments and documents
The history of aviation architecture has been studied at length in the case of airports. This study uses sources of aviation, architecture, and history to come to a first architectural history of helidromes.

Aviation sources
The sources on aviation are biased towards airplanes and airports. The Aeronautical Information Publications (AIP) are issued by each country to inform pilots about airport and airspace regulations. Airport information allows pilots to make proper arrangements and gives technical data such as location, size, approach, and radio procedures. Heliports are not always listed. For instance, in Hong Kong only two heliports with scheduled helicopter services are included while the city has many more helipads of which only the name is included. The authorities of the Netherlands have removed all information about helipads since 2003. In general, the absence of information on helidromes is more common than its presence.

The aviation sources used by helicopter pilots are sometimes published by independent organizations, such as the *Pilot's Help* booklets published for Brazil and the website www.helipad.org, which offers information about helipads in Germany, Switzerland, Austria, and parts of Italy. Their data, like the information in the AIP, are not historical.

Historical information is largely collected in the archives of the Royal Aeronautical Society in London. Their extensive library houses detailed information about helicopter-related events in aviation history. These sources have been of great value, although they were mostly concerned with Great Britain. Brazil and the Netherlands, which also appear in this study, do not have archives of this sort, and in the case of Brazil did not allow a detailed historical study. Dutch data can be collected through a combination of historical sources as discussed below.

The bias towards airports and airplanes is not limited to listings and technical data. Studies on aviation in art, literature, and architecture consistently ignore helicopters, and devote merely a footnote or a single sentence to the machine. Much historical information and material on helicopters in art need to be collected outside aviation literature.

Historical sources

The first employment of helicopters was in a military context. Historical military sources give detailed information about the history and use of helicopters. Additional literature on the wars and emergencies in which these helicopters were first employed present an accurate picture of the early years of helicopter use. Picture books rather than textbooks reveal the presence of helicopter platforms. Helicopters may be mentioned as part of a military operation, their landing platforms rarely are. Helicopter photographs are commonly taken during take-off and landing, and consequently give a first indication of the presence of helicopter platforms.

The first scheduled helicopter services received much press coverage. Archives of newspaper clippings at the Dutch Volkskrant Archive provide an overview of the Dutch helicopter services. The New York Times provides online resource material going back to the early days of helicopters, and is a primary resource for American operations. The Los Angeles Times is available digitally at the Los Angeles Public Library, if only up until 1962, and provides an important additional source for the west coast of the United States. Studies on the feasibility of scheduled helicopter services, published as government research reports, complete the picture.

Apart from helidecks on navy ships, the military has not pioneered helipads on roofs or other structures. This information is found in the history of such structures. In this case, history is cut into smaller separate histories of hospitals, lighthouses, icebreakers, cruise ships, and skyscrapers. Architecture is commonly part of these specialized studies, but the presence of helipads is not a consistent feature.

A study of British lighthouses requires literature only available in Great Britain. Inventories of cruise ships and skyscrapers are more frequently found online than on paper, and rarely include historical information. A detailed history of icebreakers is equally difficult to obtain, while hospitals are best studied individually. Online or paper resources only provide a first indication of the presence of helipads; a confirmation of their existence is best found on published (online) photographs. Amateur photographs, for instance, contain useful evidence of the presence of helidecks on cruise ships, since owners or operators do not consistently advertise these structures.

Architecture sources

A history of structures is also a history of architecture. Studies on skyscrapers, for instance, have become a popular field in city planning and architecture literature. This cannot be said of cruise ships and icebreakers, examples of naval architecture, which have been studied mostly by fans rather than academics. Information about helipads is irregular or inconsistent.

Helicopter platforms that were given particular attention by an architect appear in illustrated reviews of the architect's work. The presence of a helipad design is usually but not always acknowledged, and the words dedicated to the structure remain limited to its location and sometimes its measurement or height above ground.

The omnipresence of helipads in São Paulo has caused architecture journals in Brazil to dedicate the odd article to the topic — for instance *ProjetoDesign* and *Finestra Brasil*, both published in São Paulo. These sources in Portuguese are a rare occurrence in other languages, and provide rare information about the motivations and considerations of the architect when placing the helipad on a building.

The information in aviation, historical and architectural sources remains limited. In aviation, some organizations have published their own sources for use by pilots. Historical information has been found in archives on aviation or scattered in libraries, but mostly hidden in the history of events rather than the history of helicopters. In architecture, individual buildings or architects may attract attention to a helipad design, but the sources are mostly silent. In most cases the best source for studying helipads is the photograph. They can be found, if only sparingly, in all three of the above sources.

— Data collection and the question of definition

The disparity of time periods, locations and structures in relation to the data gathered on helidromes preclude general conclusions. The data sets collected for this study partly solve this disparity and facilitate general comments. They attempt to select locations, kinds of constructions and time periods. For such a limited body of data, insight can be developed on the use and purpose of the helidrome.

Sets of 20 films, 72 lighthouses, 30 hospitals, 15 ships allow statistical evidence, even though this is often limited to a particular country and period. Smaller sets of data that are complete or even near complete are not used for statistics. These latter sets of data do not allow any statistical conclusions to be drawn, but merely hint at possibilities or exceptions for different countries and time periods. The availability of sources determines the selection of the data sets. These sources ideally contain a combination of pictorial and written evidence. There is no definition of a helidrome at the basis of this study. Definitions are only found in the literature on aviation, and these definitions are sometimes contradictory and rarely relevant to architecture. The following definition exercises illustrate the problems of definition and the confusion that exists.

The paper helipad

A helipad is a many-splendoured thing. The many-splendoured part of things requires time and effort to discover, or so the Korean War setting of that name-sake movie drama of 1955 leads us to believe. Art or architecture studies rarely if ever give helipad definitions, aviation studies enjoy too many.

The aviation definition of a helipad is a matter of conjecture. Existing formulations contradict one another and are inconsistent. Administrators rather than historians and architects use the existing helipad definitions. Only one dimension of the helipad stands out, and it is mentioned consistently: a place for the arrival and departure of helicopters.

Helidrome is not in common usage in aviation, and is largely saved from conflicting definitions of this industry, hence the title of this study. Helidecks, pads, points, ports, and stops have been repeatedly at the mercy of administrators and planners. For example, Horonjeff and McKelvey in their planning and design manual capture four:Horonjeff & McKelvey 1994:520

> A *heliport* is an identifiable area on land or water or structures, including buildings or facilities thereon, used or intended to be used for the landing and takeoff of helicopters or other rotary-wing aircraft.
> A *helideck* is a heliport located on a floating or an offshore structure.
> A *helistop* is an area developed and used for helicopter landings and takeoffs to drop off or pick up passengers or cargo.
> A *helipad* is a paved or other surface used for parking helicopters at a heliport.

The International Civil Aviation Organization (ICAO) with its internationally used manual on heliports speaks of four rather different kinds:ICAO 1995:97

> *Elevated heliport*. An area on a raised structure on land for the arrival and departure of helicopters.
> *Helideck*. An area located on a floating or fixed structure offshore designated for use by helicopters.
> *Heliport*. An aerodrome or a defined area on a structure intended to be used wholly or in part for the arrival, departure and surface movement of helicopters.
> *Water heliport*. A heliport on water intended for use by helicopters specifically equipped and approved in relevant Flight Manuals for routine water operations or rejected take-offs on to water.

ICAO, in an introductory paragraph, states: 'the manual deals with three principal types of heliports, namely, surface level heliports, elevated heliports and helidecks which may be located on offshore installations or ships.'ICAO 1995:III Official aviation authorities, such as ICAO, have reason to define the spaces of which they speak for the implementation of regulations and (international) laws. Despite ICAO's efforts, its terminology on heliports is less than universal. The Dutch authorities (today known as IVW) distinguish *helihaven* (a literal translation of *heliport*) that is either a *heliterrein* ('heli-terrain'), which means it is located on the ground, or a *platform* in which case it is located on a building or ship. The Brazilian *Pilot's Help* speaks of *heliporto* ('heliport') and *heliponto* ('helipoint').Marques 2003 The first is defined as a place that has installations and infrastructure for the (dis)embarkation of passengers, supplies, and maintenance facilities for aircraft as well as communication via radio, parking facilities, etcetera. The helipoint just has a place for the arrival and departure of helicopters without specific facilities. This distinction hints at the frequency of helicopter landings. Branch, in his study on city planning and heliports in Los Angeles, USA, distinguishes *heliport* and *helistop* like *heliporto* and *heliponto,* but added a further subdivision of limited and unlimited use of either kind.Branch 1973

The above examples of definitions are mostly taken from countries and studies discussed in later chapters. They distinguish helidromes by their location, facilities, and frequency of use. They agree that the helidrome, whatever word is used, is there for the arrival and departure of helicopters.

On the following pages, *helicopter platform, helidrome* and *helipad* are used interchangeably in the text for any kind of helidrome. *Heliport* is mainly reserved for stand-alone helipads used for scheduled services. *Helideck* is used primarily for ships or offshore structures. Every other alternative still indicates a place for the arrival and departure of helicopters, but none of the above words are kept strictly apart.

Since definitions of helipads in architecture studies are absent, the following definitions provide an alternative for future researchers of helipads. They speak of material, space and meaning, and are intentionally ambiguous and perhaps out of place. The chapters that follow do not necessarily lead to or adhere to these definitions. The definitions are a comment on what a helidrome is or can be. For the following definitions the word *helidrome* is reserved.

A *helidrome* is:
a plane for helicopters;
a concrete division of air and building space;
a roof|floor of civil engineering;
a reinforced construction under a cleared space;
a fenced-off portion of a vacant lot.

The definition of a helipad is a paper exercise, and apart from the almost impossible task to provide an adequate definition, the historical development of helipads and different perspectives from which helipads can be studied do not call for a fixation of the object of study, but for a continuous reassessment.

Highs and lows

The elevated helicopter platform is understood to be on a raised structure or building. In aviation, elevation is defined as the number of feet above mean sea level (AMSL). Elevated platforms are distinguished by a different height, which is defined as the number of feet above ground level (AGL). While heightened platforms are perhaps more accurate, but equally confusing, it is understood that an elevated platform is a platform with a certain height.

Elevation in architecture refers to the vertical projection of, for instance, the façade of a building. To avoid this conflict of definitions, the word *elevation* without the *platform* and the expression *the elevation of* will be avoided, and an *elevated platform* is still understood to have a certain height.

The definition of ground also raises questions, when it comes to helipads. Ground level at an airport is a fixed point that is commonly found somewhere on or near the runway. Ground-based platforms are not different from elevated platforms if the ground was pinpointed on the helicopter landing zone itself. Ground-based helipads are not even understood to have no elevation, as defined in aviation, compared to the perhaps wide pastures around it. Only one hint comes from aviation definitions, and that is the presence of a structure.

A concrete slab placed on a small grass mound, originally constructed for teeing off at a golf course, is located at the Transamerica Hotel in São Paulo. The creation of the earthen mound and the placement of a concrete landing area indicate a structure that is slightly higher than the surrounding field. In aviation, this is clearly a ground-based helipad; it is placed on the ground and at ground level. Of course, it is *ground level* that is now ill-defined. Perhaps ground level should mean anything below a certain height. Le Corbusier suggested that no airport architecture should rise above three meters — in the light of the above an interesting suggestion.[Boesiger 1961:109]

Helipad architecture has given height to landing zones. The helipad at the Getty Center in Los Angeles could give height to ground-based helipads. Richard Meier created a round mound reinforced with stones that cover the sides. A moat or walking path is dug two feet down and circumvents the helipad. The mound makes up the helipad. The round landing zone consists of grass. A mass of piled up earth supports the helicopter.

It is irrelevant whether Richard Meier's helipad adheres to the definition of a ground or elevated helipad. In architecture, it is a structure. Ground-based helipads are understood to be close to the earth.

Feet in the air

In aviation, vertical distance, such as height and elevation, is mostly expressed in feet. Glider pilots and, for instance, Russian pilots consistently use metres. Horizontal distance, such as runway distance and ground visibility, is presented in metres.

In architecture, American sources give all measurements in feet or at least not in metres. British sources give measurements in metres, but in the years preceding their efforts to go metric the sources may still use feet or yards or some other measure. Most sources in other languages than English or from other than English-speaking countries use metres instead of feet.

No effort is made to choose between Anglo-aviation, Euro-horizontal, or any other group of users. A metre is roughly 3.28 feet and a foot is roughly 0.308 metres. One square metre is approximately 10.76 square feet and one square foot is about 0.0929 square metres. With these numbers in mind the freedom is created to use feet and metres interchangeably. To limit the strain on the conversion capacity of the reader, inches, yards, acres and any other measure of distance and area is avoided.

— Helicopters and helidromes in chapters

If the helicopter touches on the way a helidrome is viewed, then an understanding of the views on helicopters is a preliminary necessity. The first records of helicopters and helidromes in language and art receive an overview in Chapter 2. The discussion of helicopter imagery includes etymology, visual arts and, in particular, film. Film is one of few art forms in which helicopters have played a dominant role and the perception of helicopters in film is studied both systematically and historically.

The discussion of helicopter platforms is divided in three. The focus of Chapter 3 is on city heliports for public transportation and hospital helipads for public service. This public reason for building helidromes is connected to the earlier development of rooftop airports.

In Chapter 4, the reason for building platforms is sought in their remote location. Six degrees of remoteness are distinguished; they may predict the presence of a helidrome. Lighthouse helipads, because of their structural peculiarities, take centre stage in addition to helidecks on ships and, to a lesser extent, helidecks on oil rigs.

Chapter 5 features mostly elevated helipads that do not provide a community service, but are located on offices and hotels. Prestige becomes a probable reason for building these helidromes. The cities of São Paulo and Los Angeles are central, since they have the largest number of helipads compared to other cities. An overview of helipads on skyscrapers or the tallest buildings in the world concludes this chapter.

Each chapter includes sets of specific helipads in particular countries, cities, and on particular kinds of buildings. They allow statistical and other factual information about their location. Most of this information is summarized in tables and illustrated with photographs. But these large samples of helicopter platforms, when taken together, frustrate ready conclusions on the reasons for building helidromes. In the final chapter, locations and reasons only briefly appear. Instead, the architecture of helidromes is highlighted with a typology that explores the innovative part of helicopter platforms — structures unique in helicopter architectural history.

The helidrome does not exist without helicopters. The helidrome construction is flat to allow an unobstructed flight path for this machine. The helicopter seems inseparable from the helidrome. The image of the helicopter is not necessarily related to that of the helipad. The imagery of the helicopter is to be explored before the helicopter and helidrome can be joined or separated.

The possible connection between helicopter and helidrome imagery is explored first in language through an etymology of *helicopter, heliport*, and *helidrome*. The word *helicopter* is further observed in translation and as a topic in literature. In sculpture the helicopter appears in the work of Panamarenko, who is one of few artists interested in this machine. Finally, television and film provide a rich source of helicopter imagery. The machine's first appearance is traced to films on the Korean War, and the historical development of its imagery is analysed with the help of the James Bond film sequel.

The exploration of the helicopter in language and arts is a necessary prelude to the particular concerns and developments relating to helidromes.

— Helicopters in language and literature

The word

The *hélicoptère*, the *aerodrome*, and the *aeroport* were three patents of model aircraft dating from the second half of the nineteenth century. Failed flights and popular toys, curious compounds and misnomers have brought the words *helicopter, helidrome*, and *heliport* into English and other languages.

The history of flying machines and landing places starts with the word. The idea of rotary-wing and vertical flight is said to go back to Chinese tops, toys developed around 400 BC.[see Leishman 2000:1–12] The first idea of man-carrying vertical flight is consistently attributed to Leonardo Da Vinci (1452–1519) whose drawings of an 'aerial screw' date back to 1483 AD. The ideas of Da Vinci were not widely disseminated; his notes changed hands several times after his death and remained unused for centuries until his aerodynamic ideas were reinvented in the 1800s.

In the period 1861–1891 an aviation vocabulary was developed in which the idea of a helicopter claimed much attention. After this first period, which was sometimes referred to as 'Saint Hélice', a second period followed that became known as 'the golden age of aviation' in which helicopters no longer played a significant role. Therefore, the first popular use of the helicopter starts with the word.

The *hélicoptère* was introduced by Vicomte de Ponton d'Amécourt (1825–1888), who was one of the leading aircraft pioneers in the 1860s. In 1861, he patented the name *hélicoptère* in Britain and one year later in France for one of his flying contraptions. It consisted of two helix-shaped wings horizontally placed above each other, whose spinning should lift the machine into the air. It was a model steam-powered aircraft, but it did not generate enough lift to fly.[Leishman 2000:6] The name was derived from two Greek words: *helico-*, the genitive of *helix* meaning spiral or screw, and *pteron*, wing.

The popularity of the helicopter was not due to this machine, which never took off, but to the introduction of a toy carrying the same name. Alphonse Pénaud (1850–1880) developed many model aircraft, but named one *hélicoptère* in

1871.Anderson 1997:194 The simplicity and effectiveness of Pénaud's model turned it into a popular toy of the 1870s. As a result the *hélicoptère* entered the French and English language, but with the definition of d'Amécourt, that is, a vertical flying machine. From 1906 onwards, the name in English slowly changed to *helicopter*.see Stubelius 1960

In 1878, Orville and Wilbur Wright, aged seven and eleven, started their experimental flying machines with Pénaud's *hélicoptère*. Kelly states dramatically: Kelly 1940:3

> An event occurred which was to have much influence on the lives of Wilbur and Orville — as well as to have its effect on the whole human race ...
> It was a flying-machine, a helicopter, the invention of a Frenchman, Alphonse Pénaud. Made of cork, bamboo, and thin paper, the device weighed so little that twisted rubber bands provided all the power needed to send it aloft for a few seconds ... Not long afterward Wilbur tried to build an improvement on that toy helicopter ... To the brothers astonishment, they discovered that the bigger the machine, the less it would fly;

The *aerodrome* was a machine before it was a place. In 1893, the American scientist Samuel Pierpont Langley (1834–1906) developed a steam-powered small-scale flying machine. On 6 May 1896, he proved that heavier-than-air powered flight was possible by flying such a machine for one kilometre at seventy to one hundred feet above the Potomac River near Washington in the presence of Alexander Graham Bell.Anderson 1997:188 He named his flying machines *aerodromes*, since he had been informed that this meant 'air runner' in Greek. Later this name was dismissed as a misnomer, since it should have been applied to the place from which the machine flew rather than the flying machine itself. In this latter capacity the word entered the English and French language. Analogous to *hippodrome* and *vélodrome,* the *aerodrome* should have signified a race track on which to fly airplanes, but it took the meaning of airport as it is known today.

The *helidrome* was neither a machine nor a racetrack, and it always referred to a place for helicopters. This non-etymological compound of *heli-* (instead of helico-) and *-drome* was not used until the early 1950s.Stubelius 1960:269 The year 1953 is mentioned as the time of its earliest use, but Aslan & Freeman Architects had already designed the (unbuilt) *London International Helidrome* at Charing Cross in 1952.National Archives AN 157/204 The word is a British invention, but did not enter the English language without controversy.

In October 1951, Lord Ogmore, the British Minister of Civil Aviation, announced 'that the official term for helicopter passenger stations is to be "airstops" and it seems that the name was chosen from some seventy suggestions — including "up down" and "rotorpodio" — by an unofficial committee of "well-known men of letters".'Flight 1951:547 Despite this official announcement, British European Airways and authors in the Journal of the Helicopter Association of Great Britain still preferred *rotor-station,* and it was the Aerodrome Owners' Association that coined *helidrome* in 1952.Flight 1952:611 The Aslan & Freeman Architects are one of the first to put the term to use. Its use has remained infrequent.

The *aeroport* was named after the American Rufus Porter (1792–1884) before it referred to a harbour for planes. It was an airship designed by Porter, and it is said to have been formed from the inventor's own name. In 1849 and 1850 he published two pamphlets.[Gilman 1969] The first entitled *Aerial navigation: the practicality of traveling pleasantly and safely from New York to California in three days,* the second, *An aerial steamer, or flying ship invented by Rufus Porter.* It describes the third attempt of a dirigible model, navigable airship or manned balloon. His first aeroport was only 240 feet long, but his latter attempt, too grand and again unsuccessful, was to be an 800-foot, steam-powered dirigible for one hundred passengers.[Lipman 1968:39-48] The word 'aeroport' was not yet in use, but later references to Porter's design, such as those in the *Scientific American*, a journal that he founded, mention the word as early as 20 November 1869:[Stubelius 1960:179] 'Mr. Porter claims to have invented the main features of his aerial ship, or (as he terms it) aeroport, as early as 1820.'

Around 1868, the *port aériens* had become an expression in French, at first in the works of Guillaume de la Landelle, who had a reference to maritime vocabulary in mind.[Guilbert 1965:636] Initially, this port for aircraft was equal in size and number of passengers to Rufus's ship. By the time the airport serviced the first motorized aircraft, Rufus had been forgotten. His type of ship was named after another individual, the German Ferdinand Graf von Zeppelin (1838–1917).

The association of *port* and *harbour* created, some eighty years later, the word *heliport*. Stubelius claims that its first use dates back to 1948.[Stubelius 1960:269] His reference indeed describes the first use of the word *heliport* for the mail service of Los Angeles. An article in the Los Angeles Times in late 1947 made an earlier mention.[Miles 1947:A1] The first mention so far has been made by Bartlett, at a time that Sikorsky had just set up a 'helicopter airport' in the previous year, and that helicopter services only appeared on application forms. [Bartlett 1944:F6, American Aviation 1943b:72]

Bartlett discussed the fate of Lidice, the Czechoslovakian village that was annihilated by the Germans in the Second World War. At the School of Architecture of Columbia University in New York, the Czechoslovakian architect, Robert Podzemny, envisioned a new Lidice with a heliport to connect it to the city of Prague. This idea reached the Los Angeles Times as early as 1944. Both *heliport* and *helidrome* were first used by architects.

The article mentioned by Stubelius in American Aviation is perhaps not etymologically of primary relevance, but does mention a rare joy for helicopter noise:[American Aviation 1948:20]

> He purchased maxim silencers for the machines but has never uncrated them — people evidently like the helicopter sound when it flies over the towns.

and provides an unusual characterization of a heliport:

> But the helicopter is a marvellous vehicle. It just plops down anywhere. All but three of the 12 stops were made right inside towns on small fenced-off portions of vacant lots which have been designated by the super-name of heliports. Three landings were made on small airfields just outside the towns.

The fenced-off portion of a vacant lot, in terms of size and passengers, has always been dwarfed by the Rufus-size aeroport. Unlike *helidrome*, *heliport* remained in common usage both in the United States and in Great Britain as well as in translation in other languages.

The translation

The helicopter entered languages other than French and English in two ways: as a borrowed word or as a newly created word. When the word was borrowed it was sometimes changed in pronunciation and spelling. New words were created next to or in place of the borrowed word. Such words showed characteristic elements of helicopters identified by speakers of other languages.

The borrowed words range from Finnish *helikopteri*, Haitian *elikoptè*, Italian *elicottero*, Malgach *helikaopitera*, Tagalog *elikóptero*, Kurdish *helîqopter* and Xhosa *ihelikopta* to simply *helikopter* in Albanian, Hungarian, Indonesian, and Turkish.

The common replacement of or addition to the *helicopter* is a translation with morphemes referring to flight. In Chinese one speaks of *zhí shen ji* or 'vertical ascend machine'. In Uighur, *tik uchar* translates as 'upright flying'. One of the expressions used in Vietnamese is *máy bay lên thang* that reads as 'aircraft upward straight'. Dutch *hefschroefvliegtuig* literally means 'lift screw airplane'. The Maori word *waka whakatopa* may seem onomatopoeic, but translates as 'vehicle fly away'. It is noted that all these languages have different words for airplane and helicopter.

The sound of helicopters may be found in the occasional onomatopoeic word, such as *zibi-zibi* used in Naro, a Khoisan language. But the most elaborate words concerning sound and appearance of helicopters are found in Amerindian languages. Cayuga uses *degawadaaséhs degáadeh* that translates as 'a tornado it flies' or simply 'a flying tornado'.[Froman & Keye 2002:153] The Navajo speak of a *chidí naat'a'í bikáá' ná'ooblhí* that translates as an 'airplane on top of which something whirls rapidly'.[Young & Morgan 1987:915] In the related Western Apache language *na'idiihí biká' lhéé'ilhtlhiishí* stands for helicopter and if translated speaks of 'the animal that thunders on top that flies through the air'.[Bray 1998:366]

This sampler of helicopter synonyms presents a continuing history of the word. The world's dictionaries do not consistently contain a lemma for this machine, and languages such as Icelandic and Blackfoot only recently agreed or are still agreeing on their own word for helicopter. The characteristic elements contained in the original word are different or more elaborate in newly created words of other languages. The use of these etymologies is problematic for a cultural interpretation of the helicopter, since they are primarily linguistic constructs. The discussion of these alternative words merely helps to prevent analyses or definitions of helicopter that limit themselves to the *helix* and the *pteron*.

First literary use

Jules Verne was impressed by the design of Ponton d'Amécourt, and he joined the discussions and societies relating to the possibility of heavier-than-air flying machines.[Dumas 2000] In his *Musée de Familles* of 1863, he published his scientific studies on aviation based on the experiments conducted by d'Amécourt and de la Landelle. Franquinet adds that it was particularly the successful flights by

Front cover of *Robur-le-conquérant* by
Jules Verne depicting the *Albatross*

the Italian Enrico Forlanini (1848–1930) in Milan in 1877, who lifted a helicopter thirteen metres above ground, which convinced Jules Verne that the future of aviation was with rotary-wing aircraft.Franquinet 1942:232

In 1886, Jules Verne launched the *Albatross* in his novel *Robur-le-conquérant*. This work was widely translated, and also become known under the title *Clipper of the Clouds* in the British edition of 1887.Taves & Michaluk 1996:170

The *Albatross* can be seen as a combination of a ship and a helicopter that is powered by electricity and uses multiple propellers to lift itself into the air. Unwin 2000:48 It has an additional aft propeller that was to send it forward. The *Albatross* has become a popular image and reoccurs in Jules Verne's *Maître du Monde* of 1904. It is the first helicopter that entered the international literature.

Verne's explanations of the heavier-than-air machine, the illustrations and the use of the word *hélicoptère* fixed the machine and the word in the public's imagination. Hollywood caught on and produced *Master of the World* (1961) with Vincent Price as Robur and Charles Bronson as John Strock.Taves & Michaluk 1996:170 The plot is a combination of the books *Robur-the-conqueror* and *Master of the World*. It is not the performances of the actors but the two miniature *Albatross* models of three and ten feet long that steal the show in the film.

It was not until the helicopter went beyond its experimental stages that book authors and film producers revived or initiated their interest in helicopters. A comprehensive discussion of the helicopter in the arts consists almost exclusively of works from the second half of the twentieth century.

— Helicopters in sculpture

Unlike the swashbuckling airmen and graceful aircraft from the first half of the twentieth century, helicopters did not enter the world stage as heroes. The age of invention, discovery and heroism had disappeared from the air, and moved to space where astronauts took on the new age.[Wohl 1994] Helicopters appeared as useful machines, from speedy taxis to powerful tanks, as exemplified by their role in warfare.

When helicopters are portrayed in art, their symbolism is found in their threatening, destructive and warlike image. This is powerfully portrayed in a painting by Paolo Baratella, *Nostra Signora dei Pli* (1972) that shows military men boarding rows of helicopters with rotors filling up the sky. Peter Sorge's *Groteske III* (1972) brings a similar image in which a row of Vietnam (Huey) helicopters hits the eye. More threatening are images in which the helicopter hovers above its victims. Nikolaus Störtenbecker's *Rollbahn* (1968) shows a helicopter above the smoke of destruction, and Detlef Kappeler's *Flugobjekt 3 zu den Ereignissen in Brokdorf* (1976) portrays the helicopter above a person lying face-down underneath.

This image of a helicopter as a destruction device is also found in sculptured images. Fiona Banner's *Chinook Mobile* has the infamous Chinook war helicopters literally hovering above one's head. Pat Renick turned a helicopter OH-6A Cayuse into a *Triceracopter: the hope for the obsolescence of war*, a dinosaur machine to become extinct.

The images of helicopters in art are few. One artist stands out because of his oeuvre of aviation art, and because his helicopters do nothing to appear threatening.

Panamarenko

From 1967 until the present, Panamarenko, a Belgian artist born in 1940, has designed and built helicopters and other flying machines. He discusses in detail the preparation for his first helicopters in one of his own publications. Panamarenko's artworks have been contrasted with works of other modern artists of his time, and also with other artists who used the theme of flying in their artwork. In these comparisons and discussions, the helicopters are either not mentioned or only seen as one of a series of his so-called 'man-powered flying machines'. One of the few comparative works that include helicopter-related art does not mention Panamarenko's helicopters, but mentions his other flying machines instead.[Ruhrfestspiele 1977]

Panamarenko has produced at least five full-size helicopters. They invariably allow the pilot to power the rotors. The design is slim and light, and at first sight it seems to be a glider rather than a helicopter. This peaceful, as opposed to threatening, appearance is unique for Panamarenko's helicopter objects. The *Scimitar* has an added characteristic, since the rotors take the shape of a sable blade; in other words, the rotors are not just designed for lift, but also for character.

The latest objects by Panamarenko again include helicopter concepts. The backpack has become a theme, as is exemplified by his multiples, listed below. The *Island* uses yet another technique, that of ramjet propulsion, which was briefly used in helicopter engineering in the 1950s. The idea of an entire

Pepto Bismo by Panamarenko
← *Island* by Panamarenko

island flying with ramjet rotors takes even the aviation specialist by surprise. The contrast of Panamarenko's helicopters and those artworks using helicopters reveals a dimension of the aesthetic quality of Panamarenko's design unnoticed in previous analyses. In particular, it shows a *tour de force* on the part of the artist, since helicopters did not posses the same poetic qualities as other flying machines prior to Panamarenko. Panamarenko's helicopter is devoid of threatening or warlike attributes. It is an elegant slim design of wings, which, when the rotor is placed sideways, resembles a glider. The peacefulness of a glider is accentuated by the absence of an engine. The thin tail boom and its miniature tail rotor add to the fragile appearance.

Panamarenko speaks of helicopters and not of autogiros, for which lightweight constructions are common and for which the engine does not turn the rotors. The engine, the casing, the inner mechanics, and even the skids or wheels are absent. As such, it is not a machine, but a naked model whose shapes are elegant and slim or Utopian and poetic, as is said of many of Panamarenko's sculptures. Against the current of heroic aircraft or space machines, the sculpture exhibits only the elements of flight: an open-air cockpit with rotors whisking overhead, a single-seater conquering the sky but not the enemy.

Two elements constitute a helicopter in his design: moving rotor-wings and a possible tail rotor. A comparison with other aircraft from the mind of Panamarenko suggests that engines, mechanics and casing are ignored consistently. The sculptures capture those elements that make them aircraft — wings. The place, proportion and size of these wings are the focus of the artist.

In the last ten years, the helicopter theme has been used in designs of multiples instead of or next to objects. The portable flying machines continue to be a theme in Panamarenko's work — at least since 1969 when he designed *Portable Air Transport* — but comes with different technical solutions. The half-rotor and the rotors in different configurations have now all been tried in Panamarenko's designs, most of which are no longer or have not yet been tried in aviation.

A selection of Panamarenko's objects with helicopter theme

*   Translated from Dutch when applicable

**   R = number of rotors, B = number of blades per rotor

***   A tandem configuration has two rotors at opposite ends of the aircraft. Coaxial rotors
consist of two rotors placed on top of each other. Both designs do not require a tail rotor.

Year	Name*	Size (cm)	R (B)**	Remarks***
1967	Das Flugzeug	150×700×1600	2 (3)	man powered, tandem
1979	Helicopter Sir George Cailey	8×29.5×24.5	2 (4)	coaxial rotors
1973–1986	Helicopter	100×900	1 (2)	man powered
1988	1 Min. Heli Electric	183×90×35	1 (2)	portable, no tail rotor, folded in pouch
1990	The Helicopter	1000×2200	2 (2)	man powered, tandem
1990	Red Helicopter	150×1000×400	1 (2)	man powered
1990	Scimitar	228×1100×538	1 (2)	man powered, curved rotor blades

Latest helicopter themes in Panamarenko's objects

*   R = number of rotors, B = number of blades per rotor

**   A polyester object was turned into bronze and is permanently displayed at the St Jans Square in Antwerp. The full-size person wears a portable flying machine.

Year	Name	Size (cm)	R (B)*	Remarks
2003	Japanese Flying Pack/Pepto Bismo	200×200	6 (2)	portable, carried on back, bronze from polyester**
2004	Island	1800 Ø	1 (2)	ramjets, three passengers

Panamarenko's multiples with helicopter theme 1995–2002

*   R = number of rotors, B = number of blades per rotor

Year	Name	Art work	Size	R (B)*	Remarks
1995	Pepto Bismo	Colour print, Japanese paper	38.3×29.5	12 (2)	backpack format
1999	Zwungrad	Offset lithograph	70×50	1 (1)	man powered, backpack format
2000	Monocedo	Silk-screen print	70×70	1 (1)	floats
2001	Bernoulli II	Offset lithograph	70×50	2 (2)	under balloon
2002	Catapult Max	Colour print	25.5×25.4	2 (2)	tandem formation, backpack format

Helicopter image

Panamarenko's helicopter is part of an oeuvre of flying machines, and also part
of the man-powered machines he created. His *Japanese flying pack — Pepto
Bismo* (2003) has six small rotors placed on a backpack construction. The
rotors are placed on poles and together they create a small *Albatross* for personal use. The *Albatross* image is a futuristic image rather than one of vio-
lence and war.

The art of Panamarenko is commonly treated as a group of artworks with
common attributes of fragile materials, man-powered themes, disfunctionality,
and playfulness. A comparison of helicopter art by other artists with Panamarenko's helicopters shows a contrast of warlike and tranquil images. The
thematic contrast also highlights the aesthetic accomplishment of Panama-

renko's helicopters. While the aesthetic and poetic elements of fixed-wing aircraft and even balloons had been present in at least half a century of previous art works, the helicopter was the absent, ugly duckling of aviation. In Robert Aldrich's film *Flight of the Phoenix* (1965), Hardy Kruger plays a model airplane designer by the name of Heinrich Dorfmann who apologizes for his airplane design by stating: 'Don't worry ... helicopters don't look very elegant either, but they fly reasonably well.'

When the helicopter entered the visual arts, the artists portrayed it as a war machine, but not as the representation of the dream of flight. This is not only explained by the timing of the helicopter era, but also by its shape. The rotating wings above a lumpy cockpit with a long tail did not inspire the poetic but the horrific. Swarms of helicopters reinforced the image of war and threat, but not the romance of flight. Only Panamarenko shows otherwise.

All flying constructions by Panamarenko were made to fly. Calculations accompany the designs and some models, such as his *U-Kontrol II*, were tested at the Carnfield Institute of Technology in 1972.[Theys 1992:283] Spectators, scientists or aviators may doubt the flying possibilities, particularly since most of his models have never been taken to the air. Yet, this flying intention is consistently present. The objects are functional, but not necessarily put to use.

The functionality of Panamarenko's art can also be found in the architecture of helipads. They are a consistent, calculated possibility for helicopter landings, a design that does not refer to war, but a design that is made for helicopter landings even if these landings rarely take place.

— Helicopters on film and television

Helicopters have trailed airplanes in literature, art, and film. Television and colour film, however, became commercially viable in the 1940s and 1950s at approximately the same time as the helicopter. One of the earlier television series and colour films featured helicopters as well as airplanes, and the importance of television and film in popular culture also established the role of helicopters firmly in comparison with airplanes.

The first prime-time television series to feature helicopters in the lead role was *The Whirlybirds* (1957–1959), also known as *Copter Patrol*. With one hundred and eleven half-hour black-and-white mono-sound episodes, it gave the American public a thorough introduction to the helicopter, in particular to the Bell 47 and later the Bell J2 helicopters. Chuck Martin, played by Kenneth Toby, and Pete (P.T.) Moore, played by Craig Hill, portrayed owners of a helicopter company who would be hired out for all sorts of jobs, such as locating lost prospectors, delivering supplies, and chasing criminals. It became a substantial hit with the younger audience.[Brooks & Marsh 1988:858]

One of the most popular syndicated programmes in television history, according to Brooks & Marsh, was the television series *Highway Patrol* (1955–1959).[Brooks & Marsh 1988:343] It had motorcycles, patrol cars, and helicopters fighting crime on America's highways. With 156 half-hour black-and-white episodes, it sealed the image of helicopters on the screen — a supporting role in action scenes.

Highway Patrol was later followed by *Chopper One*, a police drama, in which two policemen were assigned to helicopter duty in a Californian city. It was a short run between January 17, 1974 and July 11, 1974.

The Bell 47 helicopter became part of the signature opening scene of M*A*S*H, one of the longest-running and most highly regarded television series of the 1970s and early 1980s. It confirmed the film image of helicopters, and it featured the medical airlift in the Korean War while the Vietnam War was still fresh in the viewers' memory. Even though it showed helicopters at the beginning of every episode, the leading characters were doctors, nurses, and patients. The helicopter pilot was limited to the occasional patient role, such as the pilot named 'Cowboy' in one of the first year episodes.Kalter 1984:42–43

In 1983 the feature film *Blue Thunder,* starring a futuristic helicopter, appears to have changed helicopter popularity. It resulted in the year of the helicopter, at least on television, since prime-time television series with helicopters were telecast on three different US television networks. *Blue Thunder*, as a television series, started on 6 January 1984 and had its last episode on 7 September 1984. 'The real star of the show, as of the movie, was the ominous black chopper.'Brooks & Marsh 1988:92 This police drama on ABC network television competed with *Airwolf* on CBS, which lasted a little longer from 22 January 1984 until 23 July 1986. It was subsequently aired on USA Cable in January 1987 with a different cast. The helicopter was equal to the one in *Blue Thunder,* but, apart from the futuristic features, could also outrace conventional jet aircraft. Finally, *Riptide* was aired on NBC from 3 January 1984 until 18 April 1986. This time, a speedboat and an 'aging but serviceable helicopter, the Screaming Mimi (a bulky Sikorsky, painted pink with a gaping mouth on the front)' was used by two private detectives.Brooks & Marsh 1988:665 The pilots turn out to be crime fighters and *Blue Thunder* and a series such as *Magnum P.I.*, which dates back to the 1980s and featured a helicopter in a secondary role, also stressed the war in Vietnam as an earlier experience of the pilots.

The helicopter rather than the pilot claims all attention. In the case of *Highway Patrol* the helicopter pilot was played by Bob Gilbreath, a true aerial stuntman and pilot; in other words, the pilot played himself.

The pilot, actor, and cameraman

The role of the helicopter pilot in films and television series was often minor or anonymous, apart from the few exceptions mentioned above, and frequently played by a pilot rather than an actor. Bob Gilbreath (1926–1961) played an uncredited helicopter pilot in the film *Ocean's Eleven* (1960) in which he also performed the stunts. He did just the stunts in *The Whirlybirds,* but made a guest appearance as a helicopter pilot in the television show *I love Lucy* (1951–1957) in episode #5.13 on 16 January 1956. Unfortunately he died in a helicopter crash, due to a fuel pump failure, near the Sequoia National Forest in California in 1961.

Gilbreath's dual career is not uncommon. Harry Hauss, who flew with Gilbreath in *The Whirlybirds,* continued his career into the nineties. Just in the 1980s and 1990s he was in the helicopter film crew at least twenty times in a range of action films, such as *Rambo III* (1988), *Robocop 3* (1993), and *Back to the Future III* (1990). As an actor he appeared as helicopter pilot another seven times in that same period, such as in *Speed* (1994), *Malibu Express* (1985), and *Best of the Best II* (1993). In this last film he was both actor and crew.

The list continues with James W. Gavin, who piloted helicopters in more than twenty films and other aircraft in more than ten others since his debut with *The Misfits* in 1961. From 1971 (in *The Andromeda Strain*) onward, he also became a helicopter actor. He continued as a pilot in more than twenty films, and acted as a pilot actor on other aircraft in at least six others. This list excludes his jobs as an aerial photographer, aerial supervisor, and other supervisory positions that he obtained when joining the director's guild.[Kasindorf 1976]

J. David Jones (1936–1997), a former Marine Corps pilot, came to California following his discharge from the service, and he brought his own helicopter. [Morgan 1985] He did few acting jobs, and, like Gavin, made his mark as an assistant director. He directed in two television series: *Airwolf* (1984) and *Magnum, P.I.* (1980). He continued as stunt and helicopter pilot in at least twenty feature films. He was later joined by Charles A. Tamburro (1946–) who has had a dual career as actor and pilot since the 1970s, and who worked with David Jones and Harry Hauss in the movie *Speed*.

Another group of pilots came together in the television series *Airwolf* where, under the supervision of David Jones, many helicopters were needed, and new pilots would gain experience. Dirk Vahle, Kevin La Rosa, Rick Shuster and Peter McKernan Jr., for instance, continued with their careers as helicopter pilots or extras starting from the 1980s, boasting similar long lists of accomplishments. Gilbreath, Hauss, Jones, and Gavin are only a few of the early and accomplished aerial cameramen and directors who also flew helicopters, and served as movie extras.[McClain 1996] They join a long list of unknown helicopter pilots of early and later years in war and film.

The first films — military pilots

Pilots have taken lead roles in films from the early days of aviation until recent times. Lists of such movies have been collected in pictorial overviews. [Farmer 1949, Skogsberg 1981] Of the long lists of aviation films, primarily *Blue Thunder* (1983) and *Wings of the Apache* (1990) feature helicopter pilots in the leading role. These pilots are featured as Vietnam veterans.

Helicopters were used on camera only a few years before they were used by cameras. Apart from documentaries, helicopters did not appear on film until the 1950s. At that time, war movies that were made about Korea first began to use helicopters. More importantly, the US armed services made the occasional helicopter available.

Making films with the help of the armed forces is not without controversy. John Wayne's *The Green Berets* (1968), which was one of the first large-scale movies about the helicopter-dominated war in Vietnam, was much criticized for the positive view it presented on the US Army in Vietnam. The army's willing co-operation was most apparent in Wayne's use of helicopters. 'When John Wayne needed wind for scenes, the army provided huge CH-53 Sikorsky helicopters to hover over the set. With the exception of documentaries, it was one of the most extensive co-operations of the armed services and Hollywood in history.'[Roberts & Olson 1995:544] The total bill presented to Wayne for the use of army personnel, equipment, Fort Benning, weapons, vehicles and helicopters was a little over 18 thousand dollars, while the eighty-seven hours of helicopter flight alone had already cost nearly twice that amount. It appeared to be all 'in the interest of public understanding of the Armed Forces'. [Fulbright 1970:120]

Sam Holden's *The Steel Helmet* (1951), set in Korea, was also supported by the military. The army then rescinded, because of unfavourable images in the film. This film does not feature helicopters, and it was shot in only eight days. [Garnham 1971:164] Perhaps because of this controversy and lack of support, Holden was not able to use helicopters. The first films showing helicopters were films about the Korean War, and their entrance is gradual and modest.

In 1952, Tay Garnett directed and Edmund Grainger produced the black-and-white film *One Minute to Zero*, a wartime drama in which the defence of an airstrip takes centre stage in the first forty minutes of the film. After about twenty-five minutes a careful observer will discern a parked helicopter in the background. A few minutes later Colonel Steve Janowski, played by Robert Mitchum, is airlifted by a small airplane, leaving the helicopter parked where it is. There was a speaking role for the jet pilot, played by William Talman, while the authentic integrated Korean combat footage and a two million dollar budget created possibilities for, but did not require, helicopter action.

The first films showing an airborne helicopter or helicopter in action did this in the context of the (medical) airlift. The black-and-white film *Battle Circus* (1953), starring Humphrey Bogart, is a 'perfunctory war story lingering in the background, touching on new medvac techniques brought about by the helicopter, but the film barely scratches the surface of the conflict, then still being fought'.[Garland 1987:34] *The Glory Brigade* (1953) deals with the interaction of Greek and American troops, and when the Greek forces return with valuable information 'American helicopters take off the survivors of both nations, who have now proved their heroism in action'.[MFB 1953] In these two early films the helicopter has a rescuing role in the background, and the helicopter pilot is considered for the leading role.

The Bridges at Toko-Ri (1954) directed by Mark Robson is based on a novel by James Michener, and it was shot only one year after the end of the war in Korea. The US Navy assisted with the production and facilitated 'a climactic helicopter rescue try for a downed Holden by chopper pilot Mickey Rooney, menaced by shadowy North Korean guerillas'.[Kagan 1974:81] The leading player is a fixed-wing pilot, played by William Holden, who is rescued twice by a helicopter pilot, played by Mickey Rooney. This hierarchy of fixed-wing pilot over helicopter pilot is common. The helicopter pilot mainly assists the hero, if he has a speaking role at all. In *Battle Taxi* (1955), Arthur Franz plays a jet pilot assigned to a helicopter rescue service with no opportunity for fighting. 'He makes the opportunity by taking unnecessary chances with his helicopter. Only when Franz crashes and is rescued by another helicopter does he realize that fighting is not the only way to contribute to a modern war effort.'[Shain 1976:175] It is not a helicopter pilot but a jet pilot forced to fly helicopters who takes the lead in the film.

This division of pilots continues in later years with few exceptions. The film *Breakout* (1975), for instance, shows a fixed-wing pilot played by Charles Bronson who tries to fly a helicopter but fails. In the end the helicopter instructor is asked to execute the prison breakout with his helicopter, but when he finds it too dangerous the fixed-wing pilot shows his courage and flies the helicopter

Korean War films and the presence of helicopters

Title	Year	Director	Helicopter action
The Steel Helmet	1951	Sam Holden	—
One Minute to Zero	1952	Tay Garnett	parked outside
Battle Circus	1953	Richard Brooks	medical evacuation
The Glory Brigade	1953	Robert Webb	troop movement
The Bridges at Toko-Ri	1954	Mark Robson	rescue of pilot
Battle Taxi	1955	Herbert L. Strock	rescues

back and forth despite his limited helicopter skills. The fixed-wing pilot is portrayed as a man who is clearly superior in courage and skill to his helicopter colleague.

The helicopter image

In the movie industry, helicopters were used for shooting film and for being shot on film. As in war, where helicopters were used for shooting and saving people, the two activities were rarely performed by the same helicopter, and had a separate history of development. The heroics of airplane pilots were repeated by aerial helicopter cameramen, but as actors their image is quite different.

In Michael Paris's study of aviation and film, it is stated: 'The "golden age" of aviation, from the beginning of the twentieth century to the 1950s, coincides almost exactly with the "golden age" of cinema.'[Paris 1995:7] In this first half of the twentieth century, pilots and their airplanes entered the visual arts. The image of the pilot developed from heroic figure in the early years to technological warrior and explorer of the skyways just before and during the Second World War.[Paris 1995:2–3, Wohl 1994]

Aviation has been studied as a genre of film, but since helicopter pilots missed the opportunity to become heroes of the screen in the early years, they rarely obtained the leading roles in later years. The visual image of the helicopter machine, on the other hand, is frequently employed by directors in most if not all genres of film in the second half of the twentieth century. At the one extreme, there is La Dolce Vita (1960) in which the opening scene shows Marcello Mastroianni as a passenger in a flying formation of helicopters carrying a statue.[Ricciardi 2000:205] At the other end, there are films such as The Puppet Masters (1994), a science-fiction film, in which the final remaining alien on earth is able to fly a helicopter through the body of an investigator played by Donald Sutherland. This alien is eventually sliced up by the tail rotor in the climactic final scenes of the film. This popularity of the helicopter image in film is in contrast with the relative absence of the helicopter image in other visual arts.

This contrast may be explained by the nature of helicopter operations. If film is considered 'more perceptual' than other visual arts — because it incorporates sound and music, multiple photographs and movement — then helicopters are perhaps better equipped to fit the screen than fit the written page or the painted canvas.[Metz 2000:409]

— Passenger James Bond

From the James Bond sequel it is possible to distil a helicopter image for a series of films. This image is taken from the portrayal of pilots, passengers, locations, and actions of the helicopter. Raymond Bellour's psychoanalysis of the airplane in Hitchcock's *North by Northwest* (1959) is not repeated here for similar scenes with helicopters.[Bellour 2000:77–192] Instead a general analysis is sought in order to identify an image that may be recognized in more than one film or genre.

For this purpose a sequel of films is chosen that allows a historical analysis. It provides similar circumstances in which helicopters may show their different supporting roles:[Arroyo 2000:VIII]

> As with genre, the expectation of a sequel is that it will be the same but different: that it will produce the same characters in a similar setting and story told in roughly the same way so audiences may experience a repetition, and ideally an intensification, of the pleasures of the original.

In James Bond films the basic formula remains remarkably consistent throughout the series.[Chapman 1999:19] Starting with *Dr. No* (1962) and continuing until *The world is not enough* (1999), James Bond covers the second half of the twentieth century with a total of twenty-one films. The clear distinctions between hero and villain, and the continuous presence of cutting-edge technology allow the analysis to include the relation between these elements and the associated visual presence of the helicopter.

James Bond films show on average four minutes and thirty seconds of helicopter footage. This includes the time in which a helicopter is heard or in view of the cameras. It excludes scenes in which the camera may have been in a helicopter, but the audience is not made aware of the helicopter's presence in sound or image.

A helicopter is found, on average, between two and three times in each Bond film. In three films (1962, 1967a, 1974, see table) helicopters are not shown at all. In two other films (1977, 1985) there are no fixed-wing aircraft. The 1962 film only features a Pan American Boeing landing in New York for ten seconds, and apart from flying saucers, the aircraft in the Bond film with David Niven (1967a) are also shown for only a few seconds in total. All other Bond films include helicopter or airplane footage of several minutes, sometimes in addition to images of spacecraft, a zeppelin (1985), balloons (1983a, 1999) and several invented flying machines, which include the autogiro 'Little Nelly' (1967b). This one-person autogiro is left out of the statistics of helicopters mentioned above, although it is referred to in the film as 'a toy helicopter'.

The roles of the pilots, passengers, locations, actions and technology show the image of helicopters in the James Bond genre, and they hint at the general image of helicopters in film in the course of the last forty years.

Pilots

The depiction of a helicopter pilot in a supporting role rather than a heroic role is confirmed in James Bond films. Most helicopter pilots in Bond films are either not in view or are men with faces unknown to the viewer. Bond is only seen once as a helicopter pilot (1981), when he takes charge of a remote-controlled helicopter in which he was trapped. In contrast, Bond is seen frequently to take over or rescue a variety of fixed-wing aircraft, including a jet plane (1964), propeller plane (1967b, 1995 two times), seaplane (1974, 1989), cargo plane (1987), and jet fighter (1997).

The remote-controlled helicopter of Blofeld (1981) is one of two instances in which a known villain is at the controls. Only the villain Largo (1983b) is also seen to fly a helicopter, and which occurs twice in that film. In the other camp, the CIA counterpart Felix Leiter is also twice at the controls (1965, 1971), and the American Draco only once (1969). Instead, the most common helicopter pilot in Bond films is a Bond girl.

It started with the female pilot Pussy Galore (1964), ally of Goldfinger, who flies fixed-wing aircraft, but who is also seen to land a helicopter that drops off Goldfinger. A few years later, Mrs Brandt (1967b) appears as the personal assistant and helicopter pilot of Mr Osato, and flies Bond to his building. Naomi (1977) is the assistant to Stromberg, and chases Bond in a helicopter. Corinne Dufour (1979) is employed by Drax industries, and she provides Bond with a scenic tour of the Drax possessions. Finally, Xenia Onatopp (1995) takes a lead role, and she flies different helicopters with different villains as her passengers. The most frequent pilots in supporting roles are women, who all appear as assistants to the villains in the film. Pussy Galore and Xenia Onatopp are the leading Bond girls in their respective films, and they are both featured as expert pilots. In this context one should also mention the character of Pam Bouvier (1989), who is the only other woman pilot in the Bond films so far, but who is not seen to fly a helicopter. Only Pussy Galore is also featured as a fixed-wing pilot, all other female pilots are exclusively associated with helicopters.

Throughout all Bond films, helicopter pilots are not associated with the hero. Instead, the pilots are unknown (men), and, if they are known, the supporting actors and actresses are playing the part. If anything the female helicopter pilot as personal assistant is a recurring theme. The absence of Bond and the presence of women at the controls are perhaps better understood in the broader context of passengers and locations.

Passengers

Helicopters do not necessarily carry passengers. They may also attack or search for people and objects. When the helicopter is used for passenger transport, the distance and speed, the arrival and departure gain relevance. The passenger is taken from one place to another to cross a distance at a certain speed. This is similar to the use of planes and automobiles. Since helicopters are not necessarily faster, do not cross larger distances and do not take larger number of passengers, the practical choice for a helicopter can be first sought in the location. If the location is difficult to reach by car, boat or plane, or cannot be reached as efficiently, then a helicopter is more practical. In all cases, the helicopter is an expensive alternative mode of transport, and, for a few locations, the more efficient alternative.

On nearly twenty occasions, Bond is featured as a passenger of a helicopter. In more than half of those instances, he is dropped off at his destination. In other cases, he is part of a search team (1965, 1999), being rescued (1995), or in a helicopter that is part of a chase (1989). Other passengers include Russian generals (1981, 1983a, 1987 being kidnapped, 1995) and Bond girls (1969, 1977, 1985, 1995, 1997, 1999) although the latter are mostly travelling together with Bond. Other known characters include the occasional non-Russian rich men such as Osato (1967b) and Sanchez (1989), the character M, when it was first played by a woman (1999), and Felix Leiter (1989) who so far appears more often at the controls.

While Bond is clearly not associated with flying a helicopter, he much enjoys the helicopter transport. The helicopter serves the hero; the servants are at the controls. Sometimes joined by Bond girls he averages one helicopter trip per film, which is four to five times as much as his Russian and other villainous counterparts together.

The helicopter may symbolize the wealth and power of its passengers. In that case, the helicopter functions as a limousine, sports car or executive jet — modes of transport that also feature frequently in Bond films. Again the choice of a helicopter is not an obvious one. Therefore, the location remains one of few possible explanations for using a helicopter.

Locations

Exotic locations are an integral part of Bond films. Images from around the world illustrate his travels. These images include Bond's arrival with an airliner at a foreign airport such as New York (1962, 1973), Rio de Janeiro (1979 by Concorde), or Nice (1983b), or a scenic tour prior to arrival in which case a small airplane or a helicopter is more useful. In the case of a helicopter or seaplane, the locations may be even more exotic. Bond's arrival on the Ganges River in India in a mariner version helicopter could have been performed with a seaplane as well. But the epitome of exotic arrivals is only reached by helicopter when it flies to the top of a cliff or snowy mountain (1969, 1999), or when it drops Bond on a skyscraper rooftop (1997), a submarine (1977), or an oil rig (1971). Such arrivals are not limited to Bond, since Bond girls and villains tend to arrive at similarly unusual locations, such as a yacht (1983b), a remote archaeological site (1989), the garden of a castle (1985), or those mountain areas (1981).

In some cases there is just the arrival of a helicopter without the passengers being known. The helicopter flying into a volcano inside a secret hatch (1967b) is just to introduce the secret exotic location of the villains rather than it is to move the actors to a new environment. In the case of the helicopter arrival on the Ganges River, Bond is not seen inside the helicopter. It is simply a view of a flying helicopter that takes the viewer along the Taj Mahal and to the crowded river. The take-off from the Ganges indicates that apparently someone disembarked when it landed, even though the landing is not in view. Shortly after the departure of the helicopter, Bond appears at a small jetty on the river bank.

Scenic arrivals above cliffs, mountains, submarines, castles, roofs, a yacht, or the coral seashore have lengthened the arrival scene from a thirty-second introduction to a two or three minute tour with a change of music in the background that suggests a moment of relaxation. This apparent peace and quiet is also found when helicopters fly in the background of the concluding film credits (1977, 1995).

Helidrome Architecture

James Bond films in the twentieth century

*   Scenes in which helicopters appear more than once are counted as separate scenes

**   No airplanes featured in the film, just zeppelin or helicopter

Title	Year	Minutes	Scenes*
Dr No	1962	0	0
From Russia with Love	1963	4.00	2
Goldfinger	1964	4.15	2
Thunderball	1965	5.44	3
Casino Royale	1967a	0	0
You Only Live Twice	1967b	7.45	6
On her Majesty's Secret Service	1969	11.25	4
Diamonds are Forever	1971	8.20	2
Live and Let Die	1973	0.40	1
The Man with the Golden Gun	1974	0	0
The Spy Who Loved Me**	1977	4.48	5
Moonraker	1979	2.35	1
For Your Eyes Only	1981	11.35	2
Octopussy	1983a	2.17	4
Never Say Never Again	1983b	1.34	3
A View to a Kill**	1985	2.26	2
The Living Daylights	1987	1.00	1
License to Kill	1989	8.46	5
Goldeneye	1995	7.43	12
Tomorrow Never Dies	1997	6.39	5
The World is not Enough	1999	6.56	7

The exotic location as a first reason to employ helicopters in Bond films may perhaps lead to occasionally peaceful and scenic pictures, but the action-filled Bond films are better known for the chase and the fight. In that context again the helicopter is present despite other options.

Action and technology

While the delivery of Bond to his exotic location is the most frequent helicopter scene in Bond films, the helicopter as an attacking vehicle claims many more minutes. With scenes between three and four minutes, helicopters have competed with a variety of machines in staging the spectacular chase and destruction scenes that are part of Bond films.

The Bond and the bad are on two opposing sides, and either side may use a helicopter for its purposes. Bond has blown up the helicopter attackers on six occasions. It starts in the first Bond film that depicts helicopters (1963). The helicopter attack in this film has been likened to Hitchcock's *North by Northwest*.[Chapman 1999:52] Bond is on foot and attacked by grenades dropped from the helicopter. He eventually shoots the pilot after which the helicopter crashes. On a second occasion he is chased by four helicopters (1967b) while flying Little Nelly. The helicopters are destroyed by the different weapons with which Little

Nelly is equipped. A third film (1977) shows him being chased by Naomi, who smiles seductively while she flies next to his speeding car. Bond, together with his Russian girl, drives into the water and destroys the helicopter with the anti-aircraft missiles from the car's roof. In 1983(a), the opening scene shows Bond on skis, and he is chased by a variety of vehicles. The first frame of the film shows a speeding helicopter followed by a view of Bond looking at a snow-covered man. The helicopter together with other men on scooters and skis chase Bond down the mountain. Bond loses his skis and fires a flare-gun into the helicopter cockpit. The cockpit is filled with red smoke, and the helicopter crashes into a mountain. In 1995, Xenia Onatopp is lowered from a helicopter to fight with Bond, but is eventually crushed when the helicopter becomes entangled in her cable and crashes. In 1997, a chain is wrapped around the tail rotor of the chaser, and, in 1999, the Bond car eliminates one helicopter while a blowing gas pipe destroys a second. This time the two helicopters were equipped with tree-cutting saws. In these last three films, James Bond is again accompanied by a Bond girl. The helicopter as a vehicle to reach different locations has now evolved into an exotic weapon of its own.

In the beginning grenades were dropped or gunshots were fired, later missiles were launched, but the helicopter as an exotic weapon had not been explored. In the 1995 chase, Bond and his girl are on a motorcycle, and are being chased by a helicopter. The helicopter chases them at a market place where the rotors are tilted far forwards slicing everything in its way while it is moving forward. This aerodynamic impossibility still makes a spectacular scene in which the rotors do not kill the people inside the helicopter during a crash, but are intended to strike people outside on the ground.

While Bond destroys the attacking helicopter on six occasions, other violent scenes use the helicopter to attack the opposing side. The helicopter becomes a logical choice when the attacks are staged near an oil rig or a mountain cliff. Such violent scenes are frequently accompanied by a rescue or last minute escape attempt. A rare chase of a helicopter and a car with villains (1989) results in the car being lifted by a giant magnet and dropped over open water. On two occasions (1971, 1977) the villains blow up a helicopter. In those cases the passengers were men that helped them in their crime, but were no longer wanted. The versatility of helicopters is clearly staged in the Bond films. Search and rescue, lift, war, and transport capabilities have been shown at length. Since these activities are typical of helicopter operations, the helicopter has become a first choice.

Action scenes and technology have developed significantly in the history of Bond films. The films use continuously updated models of helicopters. Bell helicopters dominated the first fifteen years, while Sikorsky models and the Alouette also made guest appearances. In the 1990s the Eurocopters have dominated the screen as main sponsors. This resulted in the prototype Eurocopter Tiger being centre-staged in the 1995 Bond film. In this film, the advanced technology of the stealth helicopter is stolen, and becomes the object of attention during the entire film. It is the first time that the advanced technology of the helicopter is central.

Helidrome Architecture

Image

It was in the 1990s that the choice for a helicopter was based on technology and weaponry, parts that have been continuously updated in the case of Bond cars and other aircraft. Prior to this era, helicopters appeared when the location required special transportation. In 1995, Xenia Onatopp, played by Famke Janssen, obtained the first leading role as a helicopter pilot. Her predecessors preferred fixed-wing aircraft, or had only a minor role to play. It is as if the helicopter and its pilot have finally gained the prestige previously reserved for airplanes.

The helicopter is not staged to honour its pilots but to marvel at the destination. It is a machine for the rich and powerful, with the luxury of female pilots and exotic travel. When it takes part in the chase or the fight, it is the machine that either reaches the remote hiding place of the villain or that is blown up by the hero Bond.

Its association with wealth and location makes the helicopter an interesting image for advertising, but the heroic, adventurous and exploring image of the early days of aviation is absent. Whether or not this image is justified, it does not seem to appeal to literary or visual artists in the second half of the twentieth century. Only in film is the helicopter slowly getting on (a) top.

— From helicopters to helidromes

Helicopters and helidromes meet regularly, but they do not share each other's place in art. The history of helicopters is well researched, but that of helidromes is little known. First thoughts on helidromes are taken from views on helicopters presented by artists — mostly filmmakers — and the media. In these sources the passengers take centre stage; the modest supporting role of the helicopter is quickly apparent; the stage itself is rarely in view. The sources on helicopters merely allow a study of the *possible* connection between helicopter in art and helidrome in architecture.

Helicopters did not have a golden age that established its presence in the arts. Only film and television have embraced the helicopter, and Panamarenko is one of few artists who has incorporated the helicopter into his aviation fascination.

The missing age of helicopters

While the fixed-wing, as opposed to rotary-wing, aircraft took to the sky in the first years of the twentieth century; the first controlled flight with a helicopter was not recorded until the late 1930s. In 1938, the female test pilot Hanna Reitsch performed exhibition flights of the twin-rotored FA-61, designed by Henrich Focke, inside the Berlin sports arena. It was the first fully-controlled helicopter and the first exhibition flight for a large audience. This half of the twentieth century became known as the golden age of aviation. Pilots became heroes, aircraft became recurring images in visual arts and advertising, and flying became the fulfilment of a long cherished dream. Helicopters came close, but were not part of this heroic age and took off just before this age had ended. Before helicopters were mass-produced and conducted their first successful rescue missions, the V-I and V-II rockets had hit London, and the jet and space-age had begun. When helicopters were introduced for regular transport service, the first plane had broken the sound barrier. Helicopters were showing their worth in rescue operations in the Indo-China and Korean wars, and soon afterwards the first Sputnik entered space. After large-scale helicopter operations had earned military respect during the war in Vietnam, the first landing on the moon was a fact. The possibly famous helicopter pilots such as Igor Sikorsky and Alan Bristow were dwarfed by the heroics of Douglas Bader, Chuck Yeager, and Yuri Gagarin. The helicopter was no rival for the jet and space craft. In the history of aviation, there is a no golden age for helicopters.

The absence of a helicopter age is repeated in works on aviation and the arts. One of few works that discuss the influence of aviation on literature jumps from airplanes to spacecraft, mentioning *hélicoptère* as a toy for the Wright brothers without devoting attention to the helicopter machine.Goldstein 1986:55 The visual arts in relation to aviation have been studied at length by Wohl in 1994, who has limited himself as yet to the period 1908–1918, and, for instance, in the extensive catalogue by Baumunk for the Zeppelin-Museum in Friedrichshaven in 1996. Both present endless images on airplanes, and in the latter case on space craft, but none on helicopters. Similarly, Zukowsky edited his seminal work on architecture and aviation with only one fleeting reference to helipads, and then published a second book on architecture and space travel. Zukowsky 1996, 2001 The role of helicopters in the history of aviation is marginal to or at least separate from the century of air and space machines.

Helicopters in film

The helicopter plays a secondary or supporting role in film. Helipads occur in films but are rarely remembered by the audience. The tallest helipad, at present, is located on the Library Tower in Los Angeles, and it has had the curious honour of being the first building to be demolished in *Independence Day* (1997), a film where evacuations are seen to be taking place from rooftop helipads before aliens destroy the city. The helipad physically supports the supporting role of the helicopter.

In the James Bond sequel, the helicopter is associated with important passengers taken to remote locations. Today helipads are present for accessing those remote locations but importance cannot be consistently associated with the structure. At prestigious locations helicopters may land on a lawn without a support structure or building. Helipads at some remote locations are mostly accessed by maintenance personnel rather than dignitaries. Helipads anticipate the arrival of helicopters but not necessarily the arrival of important passengers.

Panamarenko's helicopter

The helicopters by Panamarenko are made to fly but rarely do. Panamarenko provides an alternative to the war image associated with helicopters in the visual arts. While the military has played an important role in the development of helicopters, its role is negligible in the development of helipads with the possible exception of navy helidecks. Panamarenko shows flying machines without wealth, weapons, women, or exotic locations. Instead he makes backpacks, lightweight helicopters with cycling power, and islands with rotors. This world in which flying machines rarely fly, is similar to the world of helipads.

The helipad allows helicopters to land and take off, but most of the time the helipad is not in use. By definition it allows landings and take-offs, but unlike airports it does not necessarily meet helicopters every day or at all. As with Panamarenko's objects, the helipad is useful, but not necessarily put to use.

In architecture, rooftop airports preceded the rooftop helipads. The rooftop airport was only a design and part of an (unbuilt) vision on transport. The rooftop helipad was immediately feasible, and it was put to use in the early development of helicopter services. But, as the following chapter illustrates, the use of helicopters as scheduled transport is rarely successful, and these helicopters no longer occupy the roofs. Even though rooftop helipads were present during the first scheduled helicopter services, today's heliports for scheduled transportation are rarely located on roofs, if they exist at all.

'Of course architecture is the art of creating real space, whereas film is forced to work with illusions.'[Van de Ven 1978:174] Although a leap from helicopters in film and art to helidrome architecture is not just a matter of shedding illusions, the built architecture of the helidrome was preceded by the unbuilt fantasy of the rooftop airport. Before turning to the helidrome, a short review of rooftop airports illustrates the role of the transport concept, an illusion that was given to the first heliports as well. The rooftop airports, as opposed to the heliports, never left the paper or the film screen.

After rooftop airports, two kinds of helipads are explored in this chapter. In both cases the developer had a high volume of helicopter movements in mind, and they are located in or near the city. The city heliport is a building or part of a building that is used as part of a public transport system. The hospital building with its helipad is used as part of a public ambulance system. In both cases the helipad is found on the ground or on the building.

— Roof airports in architecture

The airplane had hardly taken to the air when its landing strip was projected on roofs of buildings, railway stations, and parking garages. Airport designs on rooftops littered the 1920s and 1930s, seemingly anticipating the arrival of helicopters that could make the visionary dreams come true.[see Voigt 1996]

Eugène Hénard was probably the first to imagine rooftop airplane landing zones on the streets of the future. A six-storey building with a roof the size of an apartment had to welcome flying machines whose underground hangars could be reached by elevators. Streets carried cars underneath and trains on top. This transportation concept with trains, planes, and automobiles set a trend.

Antonio Sant'Elia envisioned the transportation concept for Milan: roads in tunnels, overhead trains, and rooftop aircraft. Le Corbusier did little different for his Ville Contemporaine in 1922, a predecessor of his proposed Plan Voisin for Paris in 1925, with a central railway and road system underneath an airport. The high-rise buildings are placed on the corners. The airplanes seem to have more room to take-off and land, but they get sandwiched between the tall buildings.

The nightmare of the stunted runway and the tall obstructions on every corner of the platform were solved in another set of dreams. Charles Frobisher invented the London Rotary Elevated Airport. The idea was conceived in 1922, the patent in 1932, but the building never turned into reality. The tall runway could spin around on its axis to provide the best available wind for take-off and landing. The support structure lifted the runway above the city of London. A more complicated solution was the spoked wheel, a design already implemented on ground-based airports, which had runways along the spokes to accommodate most wind directions. H. Altvater suggested such a design on the roofs of skyscrapers in the 1930 Lehigh airport design competition. C.W. Clover envisioned the same on rooftops of slightly lower buildings at King's Cross in London in 1931. M. Basedevant created a wheel with one spoke in 1938 for the city of Paris. The one spoke could turn with the wind while the wheel rested on high-rise buildings.[Cohen 1995:69] A pamphlet on the London Airport and Marketing Centre of 1933 suggests a spoked wheel again, but also states: 'The reception

Overview of selected (unbuilt) elevated airport designs

Year	Architect	City	Description
1910	Eugène Hénard	—	roof above street
1914	Antonio Sant'Elia	Milan	terrace above trains/cars
1922	Charles Frobisher	London	rotating cantilever
1922	Le Corbusier	—	roof on central station
1923	Edward R. Armstrong	—	Seadrome
1926	Erich Kettelhut	Metropolis	tower with rooftop airport
1930	H. Altvater	Lehigh	wheel on rooftops
1931	C.W. Clover	London	wheel on rooftops
1932	André Lurçat	Paris	garage/hangar on river with roof runway
1938	M. Basedevant	Paris	one spoke wheel on rooftops

of bulk supplies from air, road, rail or canal will proceed simultaneously with the dispatch of marketed produce without mutual interference.'Central Airports 1933:6 The airport is again used as part of the city transportation system.

Seadromes designed by Edward Armstrong in 1923 placed the aircraft on the water, and in 1932 André Lurçat introduced *Aéroparis — Ile flottante,* which consisted of a car garage and aircraft hangar topped by an elongated rooftop runway. It was to be placed on the river Seine in Paris.

None of the above designs were built, except a film version of the seadrome that appeared in the popular German-British film *F.P.1 Antwortet Nicht* (1933) by Karl Hartl, and the star-shaped tower by Erich Kettelhut of 1926 with aircraft on every point of its roof famously appeared in the German silent film *Metropolis* (1927) directed by Fritz Lang. The transport fantasy built only moviedromes.

The architects

Two of the above architects lived to enjoy the ascent of the helicopter while building projects still flowed from their pen and pencils. Apart from the occasional experiment — such as Félix Del Marle's, who painted two runways above each other for an airport at Bamako, Mali, in 1949, few continued the raised airport fantasy after the Second World War.Férey 1995:76–77

Le Corbusier had designed *Une Ville Contemporaine* in 1922 for a city of three million inhabitants and with an airport of two hundred thousand square metres. This plan was incorporated into his *Plan Voisin* for the city of Paris in 1925. Le Corbusier showed his interest for the machine in his book *Vers une architecture* of 1923 and for the present study even more clearly in *Aircraft* of 1935. This latter book features seaplanes and Cierva's autogiro, a predecessor of the helicopter, but was too early to incorporate helicopters. The flaw in the rooftop airport designs was in their inability to welcome large aircraft, something Le Corbusier considered a flaw of aircraft technology. His point of view has subsequently been considered naive and arrogant.see Voigt 1996:42

In 1946, Le Corbusier reduced the modern airport to two dimensions.Boesiger 1961:109 The construction of airports was not to extend above 3 metres in height.

This change of view on airports also made him ignore the development of helicopters.

In the year of his death, 1965, he designed the Venice Hospital.[Boesiger 1965:142] At this time the helicopter had pioneered medical evacuations to hospitals in at least two wars. Peacetime operations have already shown the potential of helicopter platforms near hospitals, and rooftop helipads had been constructed and proven useful in city areas. Le Corbusier did not design the first hospital heliport of Italy, instead he proudly presented an 'autoport' and a 'gondoloport'

Frank Lloyd Wright wrote *The disappearing city* in 1932, and made a twelve square feet model of *Broadacre city* in 1934–1935. He revised and expanded his earlier book and presented *When democracy builds* in 1945, with illustrations of his Broadacre project. One year before his death in 1958, he rewrote his latest book on city architecture and published *The living city*.

Frank Lloyd Wright is one of the very few architects to design his own helicopter. Pencil sketches survive with the details of his machine, sometimes referred to by him as a 'taxi-copter'. This helicopter project was modified in 1959 to the final shape of a flying-saucer. Pfeiffer's decipherment of the sketches and notes presents the following description:[Pfeiffer 1990:263]

> The basic idea of the vehicle was that it was to run on radio beams, or radar, as Wright's note indicates, and to be self-steering. Some of his notes are difficult, if not impossible to interpret, but the final version of this helicopter shows a machine with four doors, giving access to eight seats (or more, if a larger model were needed). The machine rests in a socket device with its entrance doors level with the station platform. When all four doors are closed, the helicopter rises and goes on its course to the next socket landing, either on the ground level of a building or on a roof terrace.

By the time city transportation systems became feasible with helicopters, the visionary architects had moved to design ports for gondolas and flying saucers. While these architects have been accused of naivety and arrogance the architectural historian Wolfgang Voigt makes the following statement about the many conceived airports on top of buildings:[Voigt 1996:42]

> Late fruits of this recurrent reverie are those helicopter landing platforms on high-rises that are used only sparingly because they are so dangerous ...

He projects the impossible dream of rooftop airports on to the windmill-helicopter platform. The avalanche of rooftop helipads and safety measures presented in this study of helipads should bury this latter insight dating from the 1990s.

— City heliports

Temporary helispot

The temporary helispot is an event. It welcomes the helicopter for the occasion only. The helicopter and the event are difficult to separate. The helicopter adds drama when it introduces a celebrity passenger or when it is deployed for emergency relief. After the departure of the helicopter the helispot is dismantled, which commonly means that a few markings are removed.

The British Helicopter Advisory Board mentions fourteen regular events with temporary heliports.[BHAB 2004] They connect the temporary helidrome to hippodromes at Haydock, Cheltenham, Aintree, Epsom and Ascot, but also to the vélodromes and autodromes at Brands Hatch and Silverstone, the aerodromes at Shepton Mallet and Farnborough, and the rowing, golf, and powerboat 'dromes' elsewhere. Such events resulted in the first scheduled helicopter service in 1950 and the busiest aerodrome ever recorded.

The landings at a temporary helispot can be as singular or as frequent as at any permanent helispot. The record number of flight movements per hour and per day belongs to the temporary helispot installed every year at the Formula One Grand Prix at Silverstone, England. Two landing spots with a turn-around time per helicopter of thirty seconds have brought sixty to one hundred twenty flights per hour to the races, outperforming every airport in the world. The flight controllers use colours instead of call signs to provide faster lip service to the pilots, who, in turn, need a special briefing a few days prior to the event. The record number of flight movements in one year, as expected, lies with a permanent heliport, this time not outperforming the international airports.

The ground, paved or grass, is the most temporary helispot. The markings install and relieve it from its purpose instantaneously, allowing cars to pass and cows to graze instead. Its temporary nature is not always visible. For permanent ground helipads, a permanent structure may be created. A concrete slab is sufficient to create this effect on a grass field, while a layer of paint may do the same for any pavement. The differences are slim.

Temporary and permanent helispots are differentiated most clearly by the length of time to obtain permission for their presence. The number of flight movements has a significant role to play. While the noise of the racetrack easily overpowers that of the helicopters, noise pollution remains a critical factor in the establishment of a permanent landing place as the city heliport will illustrate.

Scheduled city transport

The city heliport is used as part of a public transportation system. It grants access to a city, as opposed to a hospital, police station or private house. The passengers do not need to own the helicopter or the landing spot nor do they need to be medical patients or have a certain profession. In this system, air taxis provide a ride on request, but the earliest city heliports envisioned a scheduled helicopter service instead, expecting high numbers of flight movements. The city airport did not start with helicopters but with seaplanes. Rooftop airport designs were not conceived with helicopters, and even rooftop landings were not pioneered by helicopters but by autogiros. Helicopters pioneered scheduled passenger services from rooftops in cities.

A scheduled helicopter passenger service started in mid-April 1947, between Logan airport and the roof of the eight-story Motor Mart garage in downtown Boston.[American Aviation 1947:15] The Skyway Corporation had applied for routes in five northern states as early as 1943: Connecticut, Massachusetts, New Hampshire, New York, and Rhode Island.[American Aviaton 1943a:46] The intra-state service to Logan Airport did not require permission from the Civil Aeronautics Board, and took an earlier start.

Earliest helicopter mail and passengers service

Sources: Scheers 1953, HAGB 1958

Country	City	Service	First year of operation
England	Dorsetshire/Peterborough/Norwich	mail	1948
	Liverpool/Cardiff	passengers	1950
Belgium	Brussels	mail	1950
	Brussels/Antwerp/Rotterdam	passengers	1953
USA	Los Angeles	mail	1947
		passengers	1954
USA	Chicago	mail	1949
		passengers	1956
USA	New York	mail/passengers	1951

The world's first officially-approved scheduled passenger service took place between the eighth and nineteenth of May 1950, and used temporary helispots servicing a special event. The British Industries Fair featured a helicopter that made two return trips daily between London and Birmingham. The helicopter took off from Harrods Sports Ground at Barnes, referred to as Barnes Rotor Station, and the main entrance of the Fair at Castle Bromwich. Due to bad weather the service did not start on the eighth but on the ninth and was flown by a single pilot, Mr K. Reed, using one Sikorsky s51 helicopter organized by Westland Aircraft Ltd and Rotor Stations Ltd in association with British European Airways.[Flight 1950:622,631,648] The first longer-term passenger service also took place in England between Liverpool and Cardiff in June 1950 operated by British European Airways (BEA), but discontinued its services again in March 1951.

Prior to these passenger services the city heliports were used for mail services, and the mail service prepared the way for passengers in Britain, the United States, and Belgium.

Mail service

In Britain, there was the West County dummy-mail service, operated by BEA, then the carriage of actual mails between Peterborough and Yarmouth during 1948, followed by the Peterborough-Norwich night-mail run.[Flight 1950:631]

In New York, mail helicopter services were proposed as early as 1943, but not granted until passenger services became introduced in 1951. In Chicago and Los Angeles mail took off in 1949 and 1947, respectively, and used the first roof-top helidecks, while in Belgium the mail service resulted in the first international helicopter service.

Los Angeles pioneered the helicopter mail service in 1947, but scheduled passengers only in 1954. The roof of the Post Office Terminal Annex in the city centre was flown to by way of the river. Most city heliport planners have chosen a river bank or high spot to reduce the noise created during the approach. In addition to the post office, smaller ground level heliports were used near the various terminals of the mail network. Later the passengers were almost

Helidrome Architecture

exclusively transported from the (sub)urban areas to the international Los Angeles airport.

Chicago had flying mail in 1949 and added passengers in 1956. The Chicago post office had an area of seventy-five by one hundred feet on the roof above the twelfth floor, a hundred meters from a branch of the Chicago river, while fixed wing airports and simple ground landing points were used elsewhere.[Cie. Hef. 1954] On April 1, 1957, a new heliport was inaugurated at Chicago's Loop, the business centre, near the lakeside. In the first twelve months of the passenger operations in Chicago, 44,276 passengers had been transported.

Sabena operated a government subsidized mail service from Brussels, Belgium.[Lucas 1966:34] In 1953, Sabena suggested a passenger and freight service that became the first international scheduled helicopter service: from Brussels to Antwerp and Rotterdam. The service was quickly expanded to routes from Brussels to Liege and Lille, and from Brussels to Maastricht, Cologne, and Bonn. Later Paris, Dortmund, and Duisburg were also added so that four countries — the Netherlands, Germany, France, and Belgium — were part of their network. The approach routes again followed canals, rivers or areas away from the cities of, for example, Eindhoven and Cologne, and only used ground-based heliports.[Dellaert 1954] The extensive network was not profitable, but the passenger schedule provided an extra service to the Sabena passengers traveling to the main airport of Brussels.

Scheduled passenger helicopter services would be operated by airlines, and in most cases serviced the main airport. In 1957, four such airlines had commenced sustained scheduled passenger operations.[HAGB 1958:11-12] Chicago Helicopter Airways, New York Airways, and Los Angeles Airways were all subsidized enterprises that started helicopter operations with mail and freight service. Sabena, in Belgium, was subsidized but ran at a loss. The Belgian operator used the helicopter enterprise as a prestige project that serviced their regular fixed-wing clients. All four operations maintained links between city centres and major airports or between airports. Even their forerunner in Boston was a service to Logan Airport.

Mail service preceded passenger services, and both services had airports as their main destination. Access routes were found on rivers and landings were spotted on the roof of the post office. Rooftops and lawns became the future support structures of helipads.

Rooftop city heliports

Rooftop airports were conceived but rarely built. Rooftop heliports are a matter of course. Early designs for a bus terminal with rooftop heliport for the Greyhound Bus Lines in 1946 were perhaps too ambitious for that time, but rooftop landings since then coincided with the first helicopter services.[Froesch & Prokosch 1946:39,80]

The first rooftop post office landing took place in Philadelphia. Eastern Air Lines pilot John M. Miller inaugurated the world's first scheduled rotary-wing air mail service by autogiro. It survived for one year, but the service discontinued after the machine tumbled off the roof onto the street below.[Holmes 1981:199] Autogiros are rotary-wing aircraft invented in the 1920s but lack the possibility of hovering as well as vertical landing and take-offs. The rotors are not

Earliest rooftop helipads

N = number of floors

Year	To	From	N	Airline company
1939	Camden Airport	Philadelphia Post Office	—	Eastern Air Lines
1947	Logan Airport	Motor Mart Garage	8	Skyway Corporation
1947	LA Airport	LA Post Office Terminal Annex	—	Los Angeles Airways
1949	Chicago	Chicago Post Office	12	Chicago Helicopter Airways
1952	Management	Port Authority Headquarters	16	New York Airways
1963	Kennedy Airport	Pan Am Building	49	New York Airways

driven by an engine, but by the airflow induced by forward speed. As soon as helicopters became operational, autogiros were no longer considered for scheduled operations.

The post offices in Los Angeles and Chicago welcomed helicopters in the late 1940s. The Boston service had used an eight-story parking garage. The authorities in New York quickly found the occasional skyscraper as their landing base.

In May 1949, a heliport was opened on the East River, Pier 41 at Gouverneur Street in New York City.[NYT 1949:58] It began operations on 18 May with an 'infuriated palm tree'. It was owned by the City of New York and in 1951 its control was taken over by the Port Authority of New York that also operated the four major commercial airports in the metropolitan area.[NYT 1951:33] A second heliport was opened on 11 June 1953 in Lower Manhattan, New York, on Pier A at the Hudson River near the Battery.[NYT 1953:29] Both heliports were at the river or partly in the river to provide an unobstructed approach.

The Port Authority Headquarters operated a rooftop landing zone on their building of sixteen stories on 111 Eight Avenue. Port Authority management used it to inspect the harbour and other places around New York City efficiently.

In 1951, first mention is made of a scheduled helicopter service for the New York City area as well as an airport link.[NYT 1951:1-2] New York Airways did not come into operation until 1953 after running a mail service for a year. Similar scheduled services were later offered from the roof of today's MetLife Building, formerly the PanAm Building, at 200 Park Avenue, New York. It was completed in 1963. Horsley's review of the building also highlights the helicopter service that was established on the roof:[Horsley 2003]

> Part of the roof, of course, is given over to major HVAC equipment and the rest was given over in 1965 to a heliport for large helicopters to whisk travelers to and from the city's airports. New York Airways offered a seven minute flight to Kennedy Airport for $7 in helicopters that carried eight passengers. It was closed in 1968 because it was not profitable, but reopened February 1977, only to close again three months later when the landing gear of a large, 30-passenger helicopter collapsed as passengers were about to board and one of its rotor blades broke off, killing four people on the heliport and a pedestrian on the street and crashed over the roof, ending the controversial, but incredibly exciting service.

Battery Heliport, on the East
River, New York City, USA
↑↑ Battersea Heliport, on the
River Thames, London, UK
← Port Authority Headquarters,
New York City, USA

Both the MetLife and Port Authority rooftop helipads are no longer in use. Their buildings still stand, but the helipads have been removed.

The New York City heliports at the riverside were the first but also two of the rare city heliports that lived up to expectations. The scheduled public helicopter service has initiated many heliport designs of which few have been built and even fewer have been successful. The far-fetched early designs of city airports with runways projected over the river Seine in Paris, revolving cantilever runways above the city of London, or connecting runways from the rooftops of skyscrapers all date from the golden age of aviation. Le Corbusier envisioned transport underneath, next to and on top of his structures, a complete urban transport design. Helicopters appeared too late to realize this early ambition, and once they did appear this grand ambition seemed largely lost. Today's heliports in London (Battersea Heliport), Paris (Héliport Paris at Issy-les-Moulineaux), and in several cities in the USA are located at or near rivers and are ground-based.

Noise and profit

The Sabena helicopter service had started modestly in August 1953 with its first freight flight followed one month later by its first passenger flight. A few months earlier, on the night of 31 January 1953, the south-west of the Netherlands had seen the first mass rescue effort by helicopters. Victims of the great flood, which had drowned the province of Zeeland, had seen an international fleet of helicopters coming to their rescue. High expectations created a heli-hype in the Netherlands.

As early as 1953 and immediately following Sabena's first flights, Almelo, Amsterdam, Arnhem, Den Haag (The Hague), Eindhoven, Haarlem, Utrecht, Vlissingen (Flushing) all requested a heliservice and a heliport with repeat request in later years, none of which were granted. In the 1960s, the Sabena operations were still running at a loss, and the service was soon discontinued to the dismay of the individual cities. On 8 October 1962, the Dutch aviation authorities required twin-engine helicopters for the city service, a measure that immediately closed down the operation in the Netherlands.Lucas 1966:124 The number of passengers had increased from 1,217 in 1953 to its high point of 5,365 in 1958 with its second highest number of 4,678 in 1962 and a drop to 2,530 passengers in 1965.Lucas 1966:132

Scheduled helicopter services from city heliports at river banks and on rooftop locations are ambitious rather than profitable, many of them receiving government subsidies to stay in operation.see Branch 1973:19

Repeated suggestions and failures of heliports at the river banks of Amsterdam continue the grand thought that helicopters can compete with trains and small aircraft.Dellaert 1954, Volkskrant 1984, Volkskrant 2002, de Jonge & Konijn 2006:6–7 In 2004, the first Amsterdam heliport was approved. It is, considering the short distances in the Netherlands and the expense of helicopter flights, again an ambitious venture.

The double helipad at Miami Airport International is a recent example, providing a possible airport-city link, but its free standing structure at the parking garage has already been abandoned as a heliport, only its offices have occupants. A similar structure in nearby downtown Fort Lauderdale, also part

Post Office Terminal Annex,
Los Angeles, USA

of a parking garage, can still be used though no regular helicopter service is
provided. 'Park and fly' has never become a successful commercial idea in an
area where the weather is mostly favourable to helicopter flights, the prices
are half of those in the Netherlands and the distances are greater without
much competition from other public transportation services.

Sir Norman Foster conceived a city heliport for London at the river Thames next
to Cannon Street Station in 1988: a free-standing cantilever structure, twenty
metres above ground, connecting the distant airports with the heart of the
financial district. The final blow to this London City Heliport was struck when
this project was shelved due to noise abatement concerns. Despite its river
location and high cantilever construction, the neighbourhood — Southwark,
located opposite the river — and the representatives of the Tower of London
feared the noise of the infuriating helicopter. Battersea Heliport, also on the
Thames, was a temporary location in 1957, but now features almost twelve
thousand flight movements a year.

The Jefferson National Memorial Competition for the city of St. Louis included
a design for helicopter landing areas in the central city.[Lipstadt 2004] It created
perhaps the largest number of unbuilt helipad designs for one location. This
helicopter transport concept became drowned by the noise of politics. For those
who wish to travel up, there is the winning 1965 Gateway Arch by Eero Saarinen
that allows a novel elevator ride into the sky.

Noise fears delayed the recent heliport Helicidade at Jaguaré in São Paulo.

Much closer to the city centre than the competing Helipark that was built in 2001, it did not provide a service to the public but to the helicopter owners. Its hangars provide room for fifty helicopters, soon to be increased to seventy. It was allowed to operate in 2003 when it could prove to the nearby school that the noise generated by approaching helicopters did not exceed that of the car traffic nearby. The approach path was to the roof of the hangar, since the ground helipad was not considered to be a proper unobstructed approach by the aviation authorities. It shrunk an ambition of city public transportation into the ultimate city parking lot for helicopter owners.

International helicopter services

Occasional niche markets give hope for future helicopter operators. The scheduled shuttle service between Nice international Airport and Monaco's heliport at Fontvieille appears profitable. This operation started in 1976 with one helicopter, and after the construction of Monaco International Heliport, located at the waterfront just outside Monaco, two helicopters were added in 1980 with a steady growth of passengers and helicopters in later years. Although known to perform other tasks apart from the shuttle service, Heli Air Monaco found an important niche market on the Côte d'Azur.

In 1985, Helsingbørg (Sweden) claimed to be the first city in the world with an international scheduled airline service using helicopters.[Gunnarsson 1999:1.2] The Helsingbørg to Copenhagen Airport service was later extended with services to Malmö and has now over forty thousand flight movements per city per year. Its claim illustrates the limited success of scheduled helicopter services. Sabena's venture of the 1950s had been forgotten and even the Monaco service of the late 1970s had not come to their attention as previous first cities with an international scheduled passenger service.

East Asia Airlines operates a successful regular helicopter service between the Macau Ferry Terminal and the Shun Tak Centre in Hong Kong, with sixteen daily flights of approximately twenty minutes. The Macau based company was established in 1990 to provide regular helicopter services, has co-operated with the Helicopter Hong Kong Ltd since 1998, and still continues its business. The Shun Tak Centre heliport is approached over water. It is, like Monaco, an international helicopter service in a specific niche market. The Macau Ferry Terminal has succeeded in implementing the transport concept that started most services in the first place. The top of the building complex is used for helicopter services; the building itself serves as passenger terminal; below, the ferries take passengers to the different parts of town. The ferries compete with helicopters on the same route. The early rooftop airport designs did not imagine this connection.

Structural distinctions of elevated city heliports

City heliports as independent structures are characterized by 'transparency and hovering lightness'. These words, used by Giedion in relation to the growth of a new architecture tradition, apply to the designs of free-standing raised platforms.[Giedion 1967:454] The structure built in Miami and Fort Lauderdale, as well as the unbuilt hovering heliport design by Sir Norman Foster in London, shows these same distinctive features. The building is supported by tall legs or

Heliport Helicidade, with hangars
for up to 70 helicopters, Jaguaré,
São Paulo, Brazil
↑↑ The Hong Kong Shun Tak
ferry terminal with helipad

Ft. Lauderdale city heliport
support construction with a
view from the upper level of
the parking garage
← Ft. Lauderdale city heliport:
aerial view
↗ Miami Heliport: front view
→ Miami Heliport: ground view
Next page: Miami Heliport: aerial
view

placed on an open steel construction that allows the space underneath the platform to be open and transparent.

The city confines the landing area. Built-up areas create turbulence near the platform, obstruct alternative landing zones, and frustrate the ideal flight path. In cases of engine failure, the helipad is a tight spot for any pilot. As a consequence two-engine helicopters have been mandatory in an increasing number of cities making helicopter operations significantly more expensive. Additional engines by themselves cannot compensate for the lack of alternative landing zones and the constrained flight paths with potentially unfavourable winds. Pilots are trained to fly into confined areas where turbulence or lack of wind requires careful operating procedures. Cutting trees, resizing platforms, and pilot training may ensure more safety than a second engine does.

While from above they appear as any helipad, the space underneath the platforms brings their support structure in full view. From ground level the structural elements dominate the view to the helipad in the shape of pillars or structural beams. At helipad level, a view commonly realized from a neighbouring building, the platform can be recognized as a helipad and its place within the surrounding structure becomes apparent. From above, all structural elements are hidden from view, and the helipad blends in with other roofs and parking spaces.

These city heliports do not require an office building underneath, one layer of offices such as in Miami or smaller and smaller layers such as in the London design are sufficient. When a city heliport is placed on top of an office building or at ground level the independent structure and its distinctive features are largely lost.

— Hospital helipads

Heliports and helipads are unwelcome in cities. They serve few but sound much. If a city features any helipad, it is commonly near a hospital, the place where sound is considered harmful, where all ground traffic is cautioned for its noise, and where one whispers in the hallway. The hospital is a common and welcome home to one of the noisiest visitors to the city. Near the hospital, to be of any use, and frequently on the roof, only metres away from the nearest ward, the helicopter lands unopposed by doctors and patients. To make matters worse, the hospital helipad, after some city heliports, is also one of the busiest landing spots for helicopters in the city.

Military mercy missions

This business of helicopter air ambulances did not become common until the 1970s. It was preceded by police and military business. The idea of helicopter rescues goes back to *Robur-le-conquérant* in which Jules Verne envisions rescues from the Arctic regions with his hélicoptère. The idea is as old as the name for the machine.

The transport of casualties by air was a military matter. Although men were transported in large numbers for military purposes as early as the siege of Paris in 1870, medical evacuations by air had to wait for motorized transport during later wars.Lam 1988 Air transport during the First World War was still limited. It was only in the Second World War, when over half a million people were transported, mainly with light fixed-wing aircraft, that this activity witnessed rapid development. In that same war, the first airlift by helicopter occurred in Burma. But, it required another war for helicopter operations to develop further.

In 1944, the United States Coast Guard deployed a helicopter to deliver plasma to survivors of an explosion aboard the destroyer *Turner.*[Bloomfield 1966:200, NYT 1944:3] It was not only the world's first plasma transport by helicopter, but also the first landing near a hospital, the one at Sandy Hook, New Jersey.

The first police helicopter in the world, a Bell 47 acquired by the New York Police in 1948, was designed for sea and land rescue.[NYT 1948a:23, 1948b:42, 1948c:52] Its first mission was to save five fishermen trapped by the tide on Coney Island. Such rescue missions were to become common in military operations where not only rescue but also medical air assistance was developed.

The French introduced two Hiller 360 helicopters in May 1950 for medical relief during the war in Indo-China, soon followed by Sikorsky S51 and S55 models.[see Ferrari & Vernet 1984:147,174-179] One of their first pilots, later to become the first female general in France, was Valérie André who was both surgeon and pilot.[André 1988] She not only pioneered medical airlifts, but also brought the medical specialist to the scene, a practice widely employed in today's civilian helicopter medical services.

The Korean War saw a large deployment of helicopters on the American side, particularly the Bell 47, which, like the Hiller 360, had the possibility to attach stretchers to the skids. By 1955, the British had forty helicopters deployed in Malaya flying twenty thousand sorties a year. Its Royal Navy had ten Sikorsky S55 helicopters, the Royal Air Force fourteen Sycamores and sixteen Whirlwinds. Their tasks were described as 'fetching, carrying, rescuing, and obtaining information'.[O'Ballance 1966:135,151]

Military and civilian helicopter rescue operations developed together. The United States Coast Guard gained full responsibility for civilian search and rescue operations at sea in 1946. Today, it also services the lighthouses and patrols the coastline. In war time, it becomes part of the US Navy and conducts military tasks at home and overseas. This system of operations resembles that of Canada, Japan and, to a certain extent, Australia.[see Hill 1972:15-16] The European system is different. In Britain, for instance, the lighthouse organizations are separate from Her Majesty's Coast Guard, and the Royal Navy and Air Force may operate next to the coast guard in sea rescues.

While air ambulance services developed in wartime and were operated by the military, the civilian peace time air ambulance required an organization whose structure differed from military operations.

Civilian operations

Van der Slikke correctly observes that medical missions in war had little to do with peace-time operations in which two other elements would be required as well.[Van der Slikke 1964] The helicopter was not only to outperform the car ambulance in comfort and speed, but also in possible medical attention to the patient during transport. The first was resolved when larger and more powerful helicopters were introduced in the 1960s, particularly the French-built Sud-Est Alouette II with a turbine engine, and its American counterpart produced by

Bell Helicopters. The distances within a country and the performance of its car ambulances explain the relative early introduction of the air ambulance in the United States and Switzerland and the much later introduction of the same in, for instance, the Netherlands. Once in place, the air ambulance has to be deployed effectively, which in the end results in an active use of hospital platforms.

The helicopter ambulance operations still differ per country. In the United States it is operated mostly as a car ambulance. The paramedics on board the helicopter assist in the quick and immediate transport of the patient. Rescue missions as opposed to ambulance services, at sea or in the mountains, are operated by the military or coast guard. In other countries, such as the Netherlands, the helicopter carries a surgeon or anaesthesiologist on board. In most cases the patient is transported by car ambulance to the hospital accompanied by the medical specialist. In most of Europe, the air ambulance prefers bringing the specialist medical doctor to the patient rather than the patient to the doctors in a hospital.

Switzerland was the first country with a civil air ambulance. The lack of coastline (and navy) is compensated by the presence of mountains (and REGA). The largest Swiss air rescue organization REGA conducts (mountain) rescue missions, air ambulance missions, and interhospital transports. In close collaboration with the Swiss Mountain Aid Foundation, REGA also assists mountain farmers by rescuing injured, trapped or dead livestock from rough terrain, or flying out fodder for cows and other cattle trapped on the alp by excess snow. An important feature of the Swiss ambulance helicopter for its mountain missions is the winch. The winch requires special training for the crew members. A winch may lower the medical doctor, an activity for which training is required. The pilot needs special training to fly with sling loads. This skill is left to the coast guard and navy in most other countries. At REGA the paramedic is a permanent member of a three-man crew, but the medical doctor is only in service for six months. Their employment is part of their medical training.[2004 REGA Lausanne, pers. comm.] They have completed anaesthesiology in their courses, but they are not yet specialists, such as the specialist trauma surgeons on Dutch helicopters.

The particularities of the service and the geography of the country determine the configuration of crew members and operation of the helicopters. The frequency and type of missions determine the number of flight movements for the hospital helipad.

The current heavy traffic to hospital pads is illustrated by the high number of flight movements, but also by some structural designs. The CHUV in Lausanne, Switzerland, and the hospital of the University of Pennsylvania in Philadelphia, USA, for instance, feature double helipads. It allows more than one helicopter to discharge patients. In the case of CHUV, the earlier twin helipads on a lower roof were moved higher up and were enlarged. In some circumstances the lower pads may be still be used as well.

Emergency needs do not explain the placement of rooftop helipads. Better access to the hospital building is not a reason to transfer a helipad from the ground to the roof. Access from ground helipads is quite sufficient when considering their high numbers, particularly in rural regions. The Memorial Regional Hospital together with the Joe DiMaggio Children's hospital in Miami,

Amenities competing for roof
space, New York City, USA
← CHUV, hospital with double
helipad, Lausanne, Switzerland

USA, the Medical Center Leeuwarden, the Netherlands and the Santa Casa Hospital in São Paulo, Brazil, are all examples of hospitals that placed their helipads on the roof of a parking garage. This indicates that access to the hospital building was a secondary concern, room for a helipad a more pressing one. The Radboud Hospital in Nijmegen, the Netherlands, featured a helipad from which patients, until recently, could not even access the hospital building. It is merely a base for the helicopter. When the helicopter moved patients to the Radboud Hospital, it made use of a nearby sports field from where the patient was moved by car ambulance to the hospital. The helipad on the roof of the University of Michigan Hospital was replaced in 2001 by a new facility with double helipads located across the road. This building, which also houses crew facilities, has a 300-feet long tunnel to deliver patients to the main building in the shortest possible time. With more anticipated traffic, a longer access route to the hospital was preferred and compensated by an underground corridor.

The general leniency towards helicopter noise at hospitals is related to its importance. The heroic image of the medical helicopter has given it more rights than the regular transport helicopter. In times of emergency, different rules apply to the welfare of hospital patients — the ones who suffer from, but may have been rescued by, this machine. Emergency needs cannot consistently explain roof helipads or the number of hospital helipads. Particularly the helipads at regional hospitals cannot be explained by pressing needs, as the following Dutch examples indicate. In other words, emergency flights conflict with noise abatement, on other issues the emergency argument is largely silent.

— From roof to hangar

The number of hospital helipads suggests that helipads are more numerous than helicopters. The Netherlands started its first trials with medical air assistance in 1995 at the VU Hospital in Amsterdam. At that time, about thirty-two helipads at hospitals could already be found on the air navigation maps along with about twenty-six small and large airfields used by aircraft in general. Yet, the Dutch featured only one ambulance helicopter. In 2004, four helicopters were permanently dedicated to medical air assistance, and similar numbers of hospital helipads and regular airfields are still to be found.

In comparison, at the start of ambulance helicopter services in the USA, around 1971, there were 274 hospital helipads. Similarly, this is a high number compared to the number of their air ambulances, but a low number compared to the number of hospitals in the USA.[Branch 1973:1]

In 2004, the Netherlands featured about thirty-one hospital platforms and around thirty-four private and corporate platforms. These numbers vary per month due to closures and new applications. At least five helipads had already been placed on hospital roofs prior to the 1995 introduction of the air ambulance. The first non-medical helipad on a roof was installed only in 2004 at Lukkien in Ede. It allows single-engine helicopter operations and is still one of few examples of its kind in Western Europe. Roof helipads have been a prerogative of hospitals, which feature eleven roofpads in 2004. All except the one in Leeuwarden were already completed in 1996.

→ Hospital Memorial West, Miami, USA
↘ Memorial Regional Hospital/ Joe DiMaggio Children's Hospital, Miami, USA
↓ Santa Casa Hospital, São Paulo, Brazil

The Dutch aviation authorities removed all information on private and corporate helipads from its aeronautical information publication (AIP) in 2003, discouraging the use of private and corporate helipads by outsiders. It clearly shows that only hospital helipads are given priority in the Netherlands.

Landings at hospital pads

The military services pioneered the helicopter air ambulance. In 1958, the military physician Haneveld reported after a United Nations mission in Lebanon. [Haneveld 1959:67] He discussed the psychological effects of being in a closed stretcher on the outside skid of a helicopter. Possible panic and claustrophobia did not recommend this typical medical helicopter arrangement of the 1950s. The transition from the daring air ambulance in war time to the same in peace time had to await a helicopter with a large cabin. Van der Slikke then suggested the larger and more powerful turbine-engined Agusta Bell 204B helicopter of the Dutch Royal Navy for hospital transport in 1964. [Van der Slikke 1964:104] That same year the first trial landing of a Dutch navy helicopter at the Dijkzigt hospital was recorded. It was the fourth type of helicopter to be deployed by the Dutch Navy, seventeen years after the Sikorsky S51 had made a landing on the Dutch aircraft carrier Karel Doorman. [Geldhof 1987:102]

From the beginning it was, therefore, not a civil air ambulance that frequented the hospital platforms in the Netherlands, but a military one. Today, the military services share the use of the hospital platform. The Medical Center Leeuwarden, for instance, had fifty-six landings in 2003. The air ambulance stationed in Groningen made only eleven of those; a German air ambulance made three. The Dutch Air Force and its three SAR (Search and Rescue) helicopters made all the other flights, and rescued people from the water or transported patients from the neighbouring Frisian Islands to Leeuwarden. As a result, at least five helicopters visited one hospital in Leeuwarden in 2003. At other hospitals, commercial helicopter companies and the occasional police helicopter have operated donor organ transports. They add another one or two helicopters to hospital helicopter operations.

When comparing the number of hospital pads to the number of helicopters, the military services change the comparison only mildly. The Royal Dutch Air force had sixty-seven helicopters in service in 2003. Thirty of those are Apache attack helicopters that only shoot people into hospital, or scare the entire city if they come near a hospital. The seventeen Cougar MK11 and thirteen heavy Chinook CH-47D not only wake most hospital patients, but are in most cases too heavy to land on the roof pads. This leaves just three SAR AB-412 and four Alouette III helicopters, the last of which are also not used for roof landings. The Royal Dutch Navy, as opposed to the Royal Dutch Air Force, has its own SAR activities, and owns twenty-one Westland Lynx helicopters. There is a budget to maintain fourteen of these, of which only about five are in service at any one time. One such Lynx helicopter is dedicated day and night to SAR activities. If one navy and two air force helicopters are operational, it brings the total contribution from military helicopters to only three. In total, including those from commercial companies, no more than ten different helicopters frequent a hospital helipad for medical purposes in the Netherlands, in contrast to at least thirty hospital landing zones.

Lukkien rooftop helipad, Ede,
The Netherlands
← VU Hospital with elevator
and hangar, Amsterdam,
The Netherlands

Military helicopters today confine themselves to sea rescues and the occasional island transport. Inland hospitals are rarely visited by the military, apart from a possible trial landing for training military or police pilots. The four medical helicopters permanently stationed at a hospital average between one and three flight movements a day. Most small regional hospitals average between one and five movements a year, such as the Ruwaard van Putten in Spijkenisse and the Koningin Beatrix Ziekenhuis in Winterswijk, which only remember one helicopter visit in 2003. Even the Talma Sionsberg Ziekenhuis in Dokkum, close to the busy Medical Center Leeuwarden, only has about four visits a year, mostly patients from the Frisian Islands up north, who are otherwise taken to Leeuwarden.

At Leeuwarden, nine of the eleven flights by the air ambulances (out of the fifty-six landings made in 2003) consisted of picking up a surgeon who had previously been dropped onsite and subsequently driven to a hospital in a car ambulance. This is common practice in the Netherlands, where the benefit of the air ambulance is found in the delivery of a qualified trauma surgeon, and where patients are rarely airlifted. Haneveld in the Netherlands but also, for instance, Skone & Mills in Britain mention that 'as a general principle, a surgical or medical team should go to the patient rather than the patient to the team'.Haneveld 1959:69, Skone & Mills 1960:363

Building hospital pads

About a third of the ninety-three Dutch general hospitals feature a helipad.CBS 2002 One third of those hospital helipads is located on the roof of a building. The number of helicopters frequenting Dutch hospitals is less than a third of the number of hospital helipads. The roof pads are the busiest of them all. The lack of accessible fields in the city puts their helipads on top of a roof. Only hospitals with trauma centres or neonatology departments are frequently visited by air ambulances. These hospitals are commonly found in the major cities.

The politics of hospital administrations and government determine the initial placement of a helipad, so that, for instance, Amsterdam has one hospital pad and The Hague two. Regional hospitals have less competition, so that financial concerns become more prominent. The one in Tiel had a local sponsor, whereas the one in Weert received a government subsidy for strengthening the roof and decided to place a helideck there at the same time. The cost of maintaining a helipad has increased with new government regulations, and platforms are sometimes discontinued for that reason. Since 1995, mergers of hospitals have become the main reason for discontinuing the helipads in Dordrecht, Zwijndrecht, and Harlingen. Zutphen lost its trauma surgeon, while the renovation of the hospital already required the landing area to be transformed into a parking space. The one in Amersfoort had similar reasons. Both hospitals had few, meaning less than five, flight movements per year.

The concerns for moving a helipad are more uniform. Meppel moved the helipad to a different location, since the area was needed for parking after the hospital had been renovated. Dokkum built on the helipad site itself, and found another ground location, whereas Leeuwarden and Twente built the new helipad on top of the structure that used the old helipad as a foundation. In Leiden, the helipad was moved twice during the long-term construction of a new hospi-

Dutch rooftop hospital helipads in 2004

City, location/name hospital (also known as)	Location	Years in operation
Amsterdam, VU	roof	1995–
Hangar	roof	1995–
Beverwijk, Rode Kruis	roof	1995–
Breda, Ignatius (Amphia)	ground	2003–
	roof	1991–2003
The Hague, Westeinde (Haaglanden)	roof	1987–
Groningen, AZG	roof	1991–
Hangar	roof	2001–
Leeuwarden, MCL	roof	2001–
	ground	1987–2001
Leiden, LUMC	roof	1995–
	roof	1985–1995
Nijmegen, Radboud	roof	2001–
Rotterdam, Medisch Centrum Rijnmond-Zuid	roof	1997–
Twente/Enschede, Medisch Spectrum Twente	roof	2004–
	ground	1991–2004
Utrecht, AZU	roof	1996–
Weert, St Jans Gasthuis	roof	1994–

tal. Initially located on the ground, it moved to the roof of the first tower before it was permanently placed on the roof of the second tower about ten years later. Only in one case did a helipad move from the roof to the ground. In Breda, the roof was used for an extension of the operating rooms, displacing the helicopter to a ground location.

Limited space puts helipads on roofs, particularly in cities where specialized facilities also add to the activities on the helipad. The presence of helipads is linked to the facilities in the hospital, but also to the wishes of the hospital administration. The areas become simply too crowded with buildings, so that even a parking garage will do as a location, merging car and helicopter needs.

One may easily discontinue a regional hospital's helipad due to the infrequent use and the increasing costs. According to those who order its construction, the helipad can potentially serve a need. This partly explains why there are more hospital pads than emergency helicopters and more ground pads than roof pads. Their relatively idle existence is motivated by the possible aid it could bring to patients. This is a recurrent theme in other areas of the world and for other kinds of helipads — idle existence motivated by the occasional use it could bring.

Hospital rooftop hangars

The building activities of hospitals and the crowded space in which they operate in the metropoles of the world have obstructed the airspace of many helipads. Trees and buildings easily obstruct ground pads, but rooftop platforms commonly rise above these problems. Yet, few of the hospital rooftop helipads have an unobstructed view in all directions.

The Netherlands, as opposed to the Americas and the rest of Europe, has allowed hangars to be built on rooftop helipads. In direct conflict with the clear and unobstructed view from the helipad, their first ambulance helicopter was stationed with a hangar on the roof of the VU Hospital in Amsterdam. The glass hangar and the elevator shaft attached to the main building give the helipad much visibility to passers-by. From each direction, the hospital can be seen to have a helipad or at least a helicopter hangar. The glass hangar allows a clear view of the yellow helicopter even when it is not in use.

Fuelling and maintenance is not allowed or even possible on the Amsterdam roof, the facility merely allows housing of the crew and the helicopter. A roof station brings few benefits. While he or she is on helicopter duty, the surgeon never assists elsewhere in the hospital. No additional use for the hospital can be derived. On the contrary, additional flights to a nearby airport are necessary to refuel the aircraft. This is compensated by the fewer flight movements necessary for picking up the surgeon after a patient has been accompanied in a car ambulance to the hospital with a helicopter base. The Medical Center Rijnmond, location South, in Rotterdam, illustrates this difference in flight movements. Its platform on the parking garage does not have a hangar, and all flights start from Rotterdam Airport which is nearby. The Dijkzigt location of this hospital still has around three hundred flight movements a year, of which three-quarters consist of picking up the surgeon who accompanied the patient in the car ambulance. This total number of flight movements is less than half the movements counted for the bases in Groningen and Amsterdam with a permanent base on top of the hospital.

While the VU could be accused of prestige-seeking ostentatious hangar-planning, the hangar concept was also followed in the case of Groningen. With a helipad installed in 1991, the management allowed a hangar and a helicopter base in 2001. This hangar features a rail-system that pulls the helicopter from its hangar, whereas the hangar itself has none of the eye-catching features found in Amsterdam. In fact, the Groningen platform and hangar is invisible from all sides when walking around or through the hospital. These two examples of helicopter hangars on top of hospital roofs are unique in the world. Dutch government officials suggest that the hangar concept will not be continued in the future, and with the frequent building plans at hospitals, the examples may soon be reduced to Dutch hospital helipad history.[IVW 2004, pers. comm.]

Structural distinction of hospital helipads — the stairs

Hospital helipads frequently feature a distinctive marking in the shape of a red cross or a capital letter H. Although their design does not necessarily differ from other helipads, the rooftop designs with patient access require an elaborate elevator or ramp construction for rolling stretchers.[de Voogt 2006]

The Lausanne double helipad shows a long ramp across the entire length of the building; it continues around the corner to the other wing of the building where it reaches the elevator. This ramp prevents any obstructions in the vicinity of the platforms. The 2004 platform installed on the Hospital Memorial West in Miami has a platform slightly raised from the roof, with a raised ramp attached in the same colour and design that runs into the nearby elevator building. On this modern building, a raised concrete structure close to the helipad

Helidrome Architecture

could apparently not be avoided. In the case of the Philadelphia University Hospital, the number of obstructing concrete buildings in the vicinity of the helipad is more extreme. Although it facilitates ramp access to elevators, it confines helicopter movements severely. The double helipad, which indicates a high number of flight movements, at least provides a wide landing space. At Hospital Santa Casa, São Paulo, Brazil, the round platform is placed on the spacious round roof of the parking garage. Here the elevator also reaches the level of the helipad, but measures not more than the size of a stretcher, blocking the view for only ten feet or less. It is one of the more modest elevator constructions reaching a helipad. Unfortunately, it is part of an area that is confined by a large number of tall buildings. It never became operational despite efforts to find an unobstructed flight path.Carlos Freire, 2006, pers. comm.

Life Center Hospital in Belo Horizonte, Brazil, has a parallel ramp and stairs construction. The steep ramp is narrow, but apart from the arm rests no concrete constructions with elevators are necessary at helipad level. The ramp leads to a lower level where elevators can be found. Unfortunately, the building design itself has not given the helipad a clear view from all sides. The Mater Dei Hospital, also in Belo Horizonte, Brazil, has a gently sloping ramp integrated in the helipad design, making armrests unnecessary. The boustrophedon slope brings the stretchers to a lower level with elevators. No structures above helipad level were necessary, showing an ideal hospital rooftop helipad construction.de Voogt 2006

Ramps require much space and elevators are expensive additions when the helipad is of a later date than the building itself. Elevators that can carry hospital beds or stretchers and that access the helipad directly are usually obstructive elements on the roof. The latest development in elevator engineering has brought a system that raises part of the helipad floor. Once the patient is moved into or from the elevator, the machine sinks to helipad level, leaving a solid flat roof behind. Hospital helipads rarely have an ideal design in terms of helicopter safety; the necessity of patient access prevented this. Future helipads that are designed prior to the construction of the hospital are obliged to solve the imperfections of today's hospital helipad access structures.

— Shifting locations

The film image of helicopters is rarely featured in the city. The remote location of the heliports on the outskirts of the city is unintended. Prestige is suppressed by medical necessity and safety regulations. Prestigious city heliports have been largely unsuccessful, and the few unnecessary hospital platforms have been at ground level and anonymous rather than prestigious. A rooftop hangar may indicate prestige, but the two examples in the Netherlands point the opposite directions.

The helipad was found on roofs as soon as helicopter services came into being. Scheduled helicopter operations are not successful and their possible prestige is outweighed by their noise and costs. They are banned to locations on the outskirts of the city where rooftop landing zones are no longer necessary or practical.

In the Netherlands, rooftop helipads on hospitals are more frequently used than

Helidrome Architecture

ground base helipads. Roof helipads are commonly found in large cities with specialized academic hospitals, whereas ground helipads are mostly found in rural areas at hospitals where helicopter landings happen only a few times a year. Hospital helipads are known to move from roof to ground and from ground to roof. This process is governed by the expansive building activities of hospitals rather than concerns of prestige or even safety.

The operations in this chapter do not require a rooftop helipad construction. Ground-based helipads or simple grass fields can and have achieved the same. The limited success of scheduled helicopter services has dismantled the rooftop helipad as a transport concept in architecture, with few exceptions.

Helipads are placed on rooftops in the city centres and on the ground or in the river when outside the built-up areas. Roofs are used for lack of space. The helipad constructions on buildings are hidden from view. The occasional ostentatious designs hint at prestigious reasons for building helipads as do the ground-based hospital helipads that appear to be rarely used. Despite these examples, prestige remains visible through the public function of the helicopter service and with the help of the helicopter itself. The machine seems to bring prestige to the helipad on arrival rather than leave it behind after departure.

The highest volume of helicopter operations is found offshore. Neither businessmen nor patients, but workmen occupy the exotic, prestigious and violent helicopter so often featured in films. They need to access a remote location.

Architecture in remote locations is seen by fewer people. The ostentation and prestige of remote helipads are limited to few observers, mostly the helicopter passengers.

In the previous chapter, passengers were patients, soldiers, and mail bags. While commercial scheduled services by helicopter have mostly failed, remote locations facilitate such services successfully, but almost exclusively for company employees. This chapter explores mountains, lighthouses, oil rigs, and ships as locations for helipads.

— Mountain rescue

Mountain and sea rescue was a prerogative of the armed forces in the first years of helicopter operations. The use of helicopters on navy ships and the employment of helicopters during the wars in Korea and Vietnam, after some initial trials during the Second World War, has given the armed forces much experience in this area.

Alpine rescue operations were pioneered in Switzerland without military objectives. In 1957 the Association of Swiss Cooperative Societies presented Swiss Air Rescue, founded only five years earlier, with a Bell 47 G2 helicopter. The helicopter with call sign HB-XAU was placed at the disposal of Hermann Geiger for rescue missions in Valais.[Geiger 1955] Geiger had invented the glacier landing for airplanes, but he soon realized that the future for mountain rescues was with helicopters. The helicopter did not need the technique of airplane glacier landings to land at difficult areas in the mountains.

With the introduction of the turbine-engine helicopter — in Europe this was the Alouette II developed by Aerospatiale — the power limitations of helicopters at high altitude became less of a problem. Today, REGA, the successor of Swiss Air Rescue, is an independent non-profit organization, which provides air ambulances for most of Switzerland without government subsidies. Air Zermatt and Air Glaciers, still run by family members of Hermann Geiger, are two smaller mountain air rescue organizations. The fleet of helicopters at these three companies covers all of Switzerland, reaching any destination within fifteen minutes.

In his autobiography Geiger shows a photograph of the HB-XAU on a makeshift helicopter platform at high altitude. The scaffolding shows the steep mountainside, the provisional solution and the utilitarian nature of his operations. This helipad, which dates from around 1956, is a rare example of a helipad on the mountainside, the slope of the landing spot being one of the few limiting factors for landing helicopters in mountain areas.

In the AIP of Switzerland the Swiss aviation authorities determined about forty mountain landing spots.[AIP, VFR AGA 3-3-1,2,3] It means that above a certain altitude, helicopters are no longer allowed to land at just any suitable landing place. Only the marked points, indicated by co-ordinates, may be used to land helicopters with the exception of landings in case of emergency. Since the introduction of the helicopter in Switzerland, the mountains have no longer been safe from air traffic. Air rescue was joined by tourist traffic and their disturbance of the peace in the mountains prompted this measure. Helicopters are allowed to land only within a four hundred metres radius of the forty-three

Scaffolding in the Massa gorge near Blattenbrig, Switzerland (Photo: courtesy of the Geiger family)

indicated spots. They lack all markings or structural reinforcements of a permanent landing spot; they are merely remote helispots on paper.

— The lighthouse

The lighthouse is built to be visible. Facing the sea, it is the light and not the house that attracts attention. The building accommodates one or more keepers with their equipment to keep the lighthouse in operation. The light beams out to ships at sea.

The building's attractiveness to future tourists was not a concern of lighthouse architects. Instead, the lighthouse design is concerned with safety: the safety of the ships passing by, the safety of the building resisting a storm, and the safety of the keepers who may live inside. As a result, the design does not seem to reach a large audience. Lighthouses are just admired for their civil engineering rather than their architecture, a perception that may apply to helidromes as well.

Great Britain enjoys one of the longest lighthouse traditions with a longstanding lighthouse board. In 1566, the organization known as Trinity House was granted authority to construct beacons and marks and signs of the sea.[Nicholson 2002:15] This organization was to oversee, build and eventually own all lighthouses of England while a second organization, the Northern Lighthouse Board, did the same for Scotland.

The activities at sea, in particular the trade routes, suffered frequently from the treacherous rocks and reefs around the British coast. At the remotest locations off and on the coast, the Trinity House built lighthouses as early as the eighteenth century.

Remoteness is directly related to the twentieth century addition of helicopter platforms at lighthouse locations in Great Britain. Each lighthouse that is located at the extremities of a land mass may be better served with a helicopter service. It reduces travel time and allows for emergency relief of keepers. Islands off the coast of Britain require boat rides to the mainland if they have a lighthouse. If the island is otherwise uninhabited, then all supplies to, and relief of, keepers requires a regular service with the mainland. The occasional island off the coast may not have a convenient port or landing spot for boats, so that helicopters also add to the safety of the transport service to the mainland. Helicopters allow for a quick and less weather-dependent service to and from these British lighthouses.

British lighthouses on land or island hardly differ from American or other European efforts. As early as 1698, lighthouses were built on rocks. These rocks or reefs of rocks were barely visible, often submerged during spring tide or just during high tide. The destruction of early building attempts by Atlantic waves bears witness to the extreme weather conditions that added to the hardship of building, maintaining and servicing such lighthouses in the centuries thereafter. The safety of the ships came first, but the engineering success was only achieved when the lighthouses weathered storms away from land, away from any visitor who should keep clear rather than approach the lighthouse location. In the words of Nicholson 'Nearly 100 years of some of the finest civil engineering to be seen, yet so often never fully appreciated because of its remoteness.'[Nicholson 2002:180]

Headlands — first degree of separation

Trinity House, according to its definitions, provides seventy-two lighthouses as opposed to beacons (eighteen), 'major floating aids' or light vessels (thirteen), and other aids to navigation that add up to a total of nearly six hundred. Their signals reach the passing ships. Their future changes with the demand. The above-mentioned figures pertain only to the year 2003.

Lighthouses stand apart from their fellow markers, since their buildings used to have occupants. The building itself towers above the surface to increase its luminary reach. Similarly, light vessels have a crew and a crow's nest on their mast with the light inside for the same purpose. Vessels are at sea and buildings are on land, yet lighthouses have several degrees of separation between land and sea.

The Trinity seventy-two are built on remote locations. Their names show their geography. Anvil Point, Beachy Head, Berry Head, Blacknore Point, Bull Point, Crowpoint, Flamborough Head, Hartland Point, Hurst Point, Mumbles Head, Nash Point, Point Lynas, St Ann's Head, St Anthony's Head, Start Point, Strumble Head, Trevose Head, they all occupy a point or head of land. The same headlands are found under the feet of Cromer, Dungeness, Lynmouth Foreland, Orfordness, Pendeen, Portland Bill, Sark, South Stack, St Catherine's, and Tater Du. Perhaps the Lizard should be added as the southernmost point of the British mainland although not technically a headland. Thus, a third of Trinity's lighthouses are located on such a dead-end where the road tumbles into the sea. Only ships may pass them by, but they wisely prevent any closer acquaintance.

Despite their location, these buildings attract attention. Engineers and those who are adventurous enough to come nearer or those who just cherish some photographs in books celebrating their beauty, all admire the architecture. The remote location presents a prime location, where the building stands out from its surroundings. The more remote, the more outstanding. Perhaps. As with helipads, sweeping thoughts about architecture do not always find support in the examples.

Hartland Point, located on a cape, was accessible by road, but the road was washed away. Today, only a narrow footpath or a helicopter ride allows access to the building.[Woodman & Wilson 2002:206] The keeper of Lynmouth Foreland found himself completely isolated from the outside world during a bad winter. Access to St Anthony's Head is so difficult that during its construction the building blocks were prepared beforehand at a different location in order to be assembled quickly once they arrived on the lighthouse spot. None of these locations attracts visitors; indeed, a visit is quite dangerous. Then South Stark can only be reached by a narrow bridge. This location appears equally remote, but attracts tourists because of its isolation.

Of all the twenty-eight locations mentioned above, seven have visitor centres: Bamburgh, Lowestoft, North Foreland, St Bee's, Southwold, and Whitby. The few that are mainland rather than headland-based have another two. Tourism and access appear hardly related. None were built for tourist purposes; more than two-thirds still do not entertain that thought.

The viewing public has been small, often restricted to the keepers of the building. The function of the lighthouse has remained. In sum, these lighthouses are purpose-built structures to which little prestige can be attached. Their reception has been too limited and today's tourist attention hardly changes that analysis.

This limited attention extends to the installation of helicopter platforms. The headland lighthouses were largely ignored when it came to helicopter services. Keepers who were resident with their families obtained supplies with relative ease; a car ride on the access road would be sufficient. Those lighthouses that did obtain helipads, such as St Anne's Head and Strumble Head, are in a different situation. Strumble Head is an island rather than a headland, even though the island is separated by only a few metres of sea. Supplies were obtained by way of a cable suspended between the island and the mainland. Some years later, a narrow footbridge replaced the cable connection. Distance and safety warranted a helipad. St Ann's Head does not require a cable or footbridge, but became the base of helicopter operations for other island lighthouses. The base required a fixed helipad location amidst the green pastures surrounding the lighthouse.

Island lighthouses — second degree of separation

Headlands may compare to dead-ends, but travel to most Trinity lighthouses does not stop at the waterside. It requires a boat ride that follows the road trip to the coast of Britain. Such trips are made by keepers, maintenance workers and, if present, other inhabitants. Their separation from supply lines is immediately apparent.

Apart from Alderney, no island lighthouse has a visitor centre. This is not surprising in the case of beacons, some also part of the Trinity seventy-two, such as Maryport, Hilbre Island, Heugh Hill, Guile Point, and Blacktail. Trinity has always considered small lighthouses, such as St Tudwal's, of secondary importance. In contrast, the larger and historic lighthouses on headlands and islands could be considered of interest.

Yet, it is the islands themselves that have gained attraction from outside visitors and not the lighthouses. The lighthouses of Farne and Longstone on Inner Farne and the islands of Coquet, Flat Holm, Skokholm and Bardsey with their namesake lighthouses all share their space with important colonies of birds. Inner Farne is a bird sanctuary and so is Flat Holm. Bardsey's light sometimes attracts birds at night and today the sole human occupants of Skokholm are ornithologists.

The lighthouses on Caldey, Alderney, and the previously mentioned St Catherine's lighthouse on the Isle of Wight are all on islands with more than a few hundred inhabitants. Even Peninnis, which is listed as a lighthouse, but never housed a keeper, is located on the most densely populated island of St Mary's in the Scilly Isles. Lundy has two lighthouses: one in the north and one in the south. It had a rich history of peculiar inhabitants, and the Landmark Trust now runs it. It features wildlife and a history of pirates and Vikings rather than famous lighthouses. One exception needs to be mentioned. Inner Farne boasts the Victorian heroine Grace Darling, the daughter of a lighthouse keeper, who, with her father, helped save some sailors who had been shipwrecked near the lighthouse. Her heroics are part of the Inner Farne tourist package. The story has everything to do with the lighthouse, but hardly anything with the building or its architecture. Where the lighthouse is remote, the surrounding birds attract more attention than the building, while other islands have the people joining its solitary life. In addition to twenty-eight headland locations, another twelve island lighthouses neither gain nor lose visitors or prestige, because of their location. Their audience is as remote as the lighthouse itself.

Separation in terms of distance does not predict the presence of helipads. It is the safety of the keepers that seems to be at stake. Their supplies and relief needs guarantee. Permanent resident keepers require regular supplies. Inhabited islands are usually sufficiently equipped to deal with emergencies without a regular helicopter service. But, the island of Skokholm appeared too isolated and a helipad was installed next to the lighthouse to supply and relieve the keepers. Lundy was equipped with a helipad for the southern lighthouse; a piece of rock had been flattened, since it obstructed the light of the lighthouse and subsequently was turned into a helipad. The grass next to the northern lighthouse was used. In emergencies, most islands allow helicopter landings on their flat green pastures. Helicopters are called in from the military. The inhabitants of the Isle of Wight had an arrangement early on with the Royal Navy helicopters in case of emergency. After trial landings in 1955 they made eighteen flights between 1956 and 1959 from the island to five different hospitals on the mainland.Skone & Mills 1960:363–364 Such rescue missions involved the entire island population: tourists (six out of these eighteen) and inhabitants. Regular supplies were sent in by boat.

Rock island lighthouses — third degree of separation
Rock islands are uninhabited or, more precisely, uninhabitable. Boats pass only at a distance, and mooring a boat with supplies may present frequent danger from weather and rock. The size and accommodation of their lighthouses prevent a large or any audience, and they allow only keepers and maintenance personnel to come near. Rock islands demand a boat and daring.

Helidrome Architecture

Round Island landed a lighthouse on top of its rock. Its only access from below is a flight of steps cut into the solid stone. The rock face made the construction of the lighthouse arduous, considering that this took place in 1887.

Granite rock is also the ground of Godevry. The lighthouse joined the many birds on the rock in 1859. The largest of its series of rocks sticking out from the sea received a twenty-six-metre octagonal tower made from rubble stone and mortar with a nearby cottage for the keepers.

In 1839, South Bishop lighthouse was completed on a rock in St George's Channel near Pembrokeshire. It is on the migration route of several bird species, and their attraction to the light caused many of them to crash into the building. The Royal Society for the Protection of Birds built bird perches around the lantern to reduce the number of flight accidents.

The Casquets lighthouse consists of three light towers dating back to 1724. The relatively large building barely fits the rock. It is the larger rock chosen from the infamous series of ship wreckers nearby.

In 1717, William Trench erected the Skerries lighthouse, known for the ruin that it caused its first owner and the riches that it brought its last private owner. The island has a number of possible sites for a lighthouse, since the rocks are somewhat larger and greener than those mentioned above.

All five rock island lighthouses mentioned above feature a helipad. Boat landings are awkward, since the weather is frequently rough. Keepers rarely live with their families at these rock stations. A group of three or four keepers alternate for a number of months, leaving a minimum of two keepers at any time. Suddenly, the relief of keepers added to the concerns of Trinity House. Other islands occasionally had a similar arrangement, such as Flat Holm Island. Relief of keepers from inaccessible rock islands require boat trips to be dependable or at least regular. The necessity of managing time, safety and distance welcomed the help of helipads once helicopter services became available.

Rock islands were a priority for the helicopter service that became available to Trinity House. Headlands and green islands allowed helicopter landings without much prior arrangement. Rocks had to be flattened or parts of the lighthouse building had to be sacrificed, such as one tower of the Casquets lighthouse.

The necessity of helicopters increased when less space was available for building lighthouses and helipads. With each degree of separation and with each added difficulty to obtain regular supplies, the lighthouse offered less space to land either boats or helicopters.

Reef towers — fourth degree of separation

Rock lighthouses occur on rock islands and reefs. The lighthouse of Trwyn Du is built on rocks but is still connected to the mainland at low tide; the rock lighthouses are only surrounded by sea. The situation for architect, keeper and supplier changes when the building is partly submerged during spring tide, high tide, or most of the tide. Temporary islands that stick out their tongue, when it is too late for ships to observe them, have been a menace since the earliest days of British seafaring. The suggestion of building a lighthouse on a reef that is too dangerous to approach by boat is remarkable, particularly in 1698.

The design of a lighthouse was no longer a tower of any sort. Engineers and architects thought of constructions that could weather the storms. Of all lighthouse designers and engineers, the pioneers of reef lighthouses acquired most fame and prestige, at least in Britain. Their architecture is widely revered; their stories are told and retold. Yet, few tourists ever visit their accomplishments or can see their work even from a distance. Visual artists of the past generations provided paintings, posters, postcards and postage stamps that reach the eye even today. The audience is left with a two-dimensional view that in itself is a source of prestige, since few other lighthouses receive this much attention in the arts.

Architectural innovation came from John Smeaton, James Walker, the Douglass and the Stevenson families. They were associated mainly with the building of rock lighthouses, introducing techniques for building lighthouse towers in places where the public cannot see or admire their constructs.

In 1756 a Yorkshireman, John Smeaton, decided to construct a tower based on the shape of an English Oak tree. According to Smeaton the design would be stronger, if he replaced the previously destroyed wooden structure with a stone one. The lighthouse is known as Eddystone. Granite, the material of the Eddystone reef, was used for the foundations and facing, and Smeaton invented a quick drying cement to combat the continuous flooding of the building site. Dovetail joints and marble dowels became the trademark of this and later rock lighthouses developed by Smeaton and his successors. Smeaton's tower was completed and lit in 1759. In the 1870s cracks appeared in the rock and the lighthouse was taken apart and partly reinstated on shore in commemoration of the architect. In 1877, with new techniques partly stemming from the ideas of Robert Stevenson, the architect Douglass started a new tower using larger stones, dovetailed not only to each other on all sides but also to the courses above and below.

In 1861, Wolf Rock had been built by James Walker. He added a measure that prevented the waves from breaking up the cement in the exposed joints; the upper surface of each stone was given a wide rabbet and the stone above was fitted into the recess so that the horizontal joint between the two was covered by the outer fillet, thereby protecting it completely. This practice was followed throughout all the courses to a height of 11.8 metres, and the security thus obtained is reflected by the strength of the tower today.Woodman & Wilson 2002

The helicopter platforms were installed about one hundred years later. Monkstone and many of the tower lighthouses of the Northern Lighthouse Board featured a helipad next to the tower, which was accessible during low tide. The continuous dangers of the sea at Bishop and Wolf Rock as well as Eddystone and others on the south-western coast prohibited such a solution. In the early 1970s, after wind tunnel tests and trial helicopter runs on land by Bristow Helicopters, Wolf Rock installed the first rock lighthouse helipad on top of a lantern.

The helideck required 'ingenious engineering'. Woodman & Wilson 2002:34 The steel support structure was draped over the lantern, but was not to interfere with the light itself. The wind tunnel tests had to ascertain the pressure on the entire lighthouse structure due to the plane on top that was subsequently made of a grid. This metal lace-work allowed air to pass more freely. Horizontal plating

Wolf Rock after 1973 (Photo: courtesy of Trinity House)

← Wolf Rock before 1973 (Photo: courtesy of Trinity House)

↙ Bishop Rock (Photo: courtesy of Trinity House)

↓ The Smalls (Photo: courtesy of Trinity House)

→ Needles (Photo: courtesy of Trinity House)

was fitted with sacrificial bolts that detached in times of storms to relieve the forces and strains on the entire building. With the frequency of bad weather, the refitting of plating became a common occurrence. The helidrome had risen to the top — its only safe and suitable place.

Nicholson repeatedly expresses doubt that the helipad is an addition to the aesthetics of the rock lighthouse.[Nicholson 2002] A proud stamp of a rock lighthouse with helipad from England and one from Ireland with one of their lighthouses featuring a helipad on top (their only one) perhaps shows otherwise. These flat images are the closest view and clearest signals of appreciation for most outsiders.

Artificial islands — fifth degree of separation

The Nab Tower is a remnant of the Admiralty's fear of German U-boats. Its construction started on two cylindrical steel towers, forty feet in diameter, to be sunk in the English Channel to close it for enemy ships. This plan was never put into action, and in 1920 one of these towers replaced the Nab Light Vessel. It was staffed as an off-shore lighthouse and automated in 1983 with a helicopter platform fitted on top. The steel and concrete construction was built on shore and paddled to its present location. The light shares the space on top with the helipad.

In the second half of the twentieth century, techniques were developed to drill for oil in the middle of the oceans. This development had two effects on the English lighthouses. The Royal Sovereign became the first and only Trinity House lighthouse built without an underlying reef or island; it merely stood on a long pole in the middle of the water. Then B1D Dowsing replaced one of Trinity's light vessels. In 1991, this oil platform in the middle of the Amythesist gas exploration field took over the tasks of a previous light vessel, and it brought the lighthouse as far into the sea as the oil platforms had already ventured some years before.

As with oil platforms, these lighthouses did not see visitors. Their design is considered an engineering accomplishment rather than an advance in aesthetics. Nevertheless, the late introduction of these lighthouses changed the way in which helicopter platforms were to be integrated. The Royal Sovereign's design consisted of one large flat helicopter platform on top of a pole. Directly underneath this wide platform was a layer with living and office space. The light was a separate building placed on the corner of the platform, similar to the one found on the Nab Tower. The platform on top of a lighthouse changed to a lighthouse on top of a platform.

Automation — sixth degree of separation

At first the lighthouse is removed from sight by road then by sea. The sea allows islands but uninhabited rock islands make regular visits rare. Reefs of rocks even prohibit approaches by boat unless an emergency warrants the risk. The last two lighthouses described allow ships to come near but they are far removed from any land or hint of rock. The buildings have become detached from visitors, tourists, and other spectators.

Lighthouse keepers and ships always kept a lookout on and for the lighthouse. The last decades of the twentieth century witnessed the introduction of modern

Nab tower (Photo: courtesy
of Trinity House)
←← Wolf Rock helipad with
opened trap door (Photo: courtesy
of Trinity House)
← Eddystone lighthouse
(Photo: courtesy of Trinity House)

Lighthouse helipads and automation

* Nicholas Douglass was the father of James and William Douglass

\# Number of years between helideck construction and automation

Name	Engineer or architect *	Completed in	Helideck added in	Automated in	Years #
Wolf Rock	J. Walker	1870	1973	1988	15
Longships	W. Douglass	1873	1974	1988	14
Bishop Rock	J. Douglass	1887	1976	1992	16
The Smalls	J. Walker	1861	1978	1986	8
Les Hanois	N. Douglass	1862	1979	1996	17
Eddystone	J. Douglass	1882	1980	1982	2
Needles	J. Walker	1859	1987	1994	7

navigation systems that no longer require the services of lighthouses and even outperform their signals. The trade ships have lost interest in the lighthouse while Trinity House lost interest in keeping them staffed. It was decided that the lighthouse might still have a function for those ships not equipped with the latest systems and that the signals should remain in place. Automation of rock lighthouses cut costs, while the lighthouse service reduced its role in international seafaring. Ships and staff were removed from the faraway lighthouse, increasing its symbolic rather than its practical function in the present seas. The helipad was caught in the middle.

The helicopter was introduced for the safe relief of keepers and consistent replenishment of their supplies. With the towers, the helipads would rise above the sea; they went from settling on the pasture of islands, to finding a place on the rock islands and occupying a roof, to a place above the lantern on top of the reefs where high seas or high tide made any other footing impossible. The dangerous reefs required the helipad to top the light, covering for what had been the highest point for centuries. In the end, the helipad took the entire lighthouse as its platform when the Royal Sovereign was built.

Safety of the men inside the lighthouse had brought helicopters to the lighthouse. This service did not start until 1969.[Woodman & Wilson 2002:34] Wolf Rock received worldwide fame as the first rock lighthouse to have a helipad constructed on top of the lantern. It relieved its first keepers by winch on November 3, 1973, a reminder of the first helicopter coming to the aid of the Wolf Rock keepers in the 1940s when supplies were delivered by Alan Bristow, also using a winch, but without the benefits of a helideck, favourable weather, or a high performance helicopter.

The helicopter platform had only a few years to serve the keepers' safety, as on 18 May 1982, Eddystone was the first Trinity House rock lighthouse to be automated. The years 1973 and 1982 may not seem close together. But the helipad on Eddystone was constructed largely for the automated lighthouse. The safety of keepers was no longer the main reason for helideck construction. On 21 July 1981 the keepers of Eddystone were relieved and a temporary light vessel replaced the lighthouse service, while in October 1980 the helideck had become operational. The helideck quickly became merely a landing spot for the construction men and later the service men. The latter still drop in a few times each year to change a light bulb.

Wolf Rock was automated in 1988, providing fifteen years of service to the keepers. Les Hanois featured a helipad as early as 1979 and was not automated until 1996, the helipad longest in service for the purpose of the keepers' safety. Automation had relieved the keepers just when helicopters had made it more agreeable.

By the time the lighthouses had become symbols of safety, both ship and staff no longer kept an eye on their landmark buildings.

Structural distinction of the lighthouse helipads — the trap door

The size of the lantern helideck is no more than nine metres as opposed to fourteen to eighteen metres on an average rooftop deck in cities. Elevators, ramps and even stairways cannot be added to the platform. Two hatches near the centre of the helideck provide the only access, while waiting room is provided near the lantern below.

The flight path is unobstructed. Engine failures endanger the helicopter, but the absence of buildings in the vicinity limits the risks. The exposure to the elements eliminates what is known as the in-ground effect during landing and take-off. The helicopter requires less power in a hover when it rests on the air cushion created by the downwash of the rotors. On an exposed platform this cushion is simply blown away. Helicopter landings in the middle of the ocean require additional training, specialized flying procedures and preferably a high-performance helicopter.

Most of the Trinity House helipads were added to an existent structure. Only the Royal Sovereign was built as a lighthouse with helipad included. Here the helipad has a floor the size of all the offices combined. The helipads added to existing rock lighthouses were not only much smaller, but required ingenious mace-like steel constructions to attach them to the lantern without obstructing the light.

The grid-like structure of the pad was installed in preference to a painted smooth surface due to the rough winds and the general exposure of these pads in the middle of the ocean. The decapitated original building needs to control the forces that threaten to lift the roof from the tower. Wind tunnel tests at the request of Trinity House indicate that a perforated platform allows an upstream of air to flow freely through the platform. This significantly reduces the stress factors involved.[Cowdrey & Bryer 1973] Later, tiles were placed on the platforms for the comfort of personnel, but these tiles can be blown off the platform when the upward forces are too severe, so that the platform is never in danger of being lifted off the lighthouse.

The two hatches or trap doors near the centre of the helideck indicate that passengers, fire men or any other personnel cannot be near the helicopter during landing or take-off. The helicopter has no alternative landing zone in the vicinity and the lighthouse roof area is exposed to the elements, small and without assistance in case of emergency. It has made the lighthouse helipads the most daring helicopter landing zones in operation.

— The oil platform

Helipads for lighthouses and oil platforms seem similar. They are positioned in the middle of the seas, they facilitate personnel transport, and civil engineers construct them. But, the lantern-deck is small and its flight movements are few. The offshore industry helipad mainly differs in the size of the construction and the volume of transport it facilitates.

The Gulf of Mexico offshore helicopter operations carried 3,088,865 passengers in the year 2002. These operations used 1,564,362 flights of an average of fifteen minutes each with a fleet of 625 helicopters; in other words, 2,503 flights per aircraft per year carried 4,942 passengers per helicopter per year. Helicopters in the offshore industry are today's company bus drivers of the coastal seas.[HSAC 2004]

The demands for oil and gas after the Second World War coincided with the increased application of helicopters in transport. Petroleum Helicopters assisted the seismograph crews in the Louisiana marsh and swampland as early as 1949. They acquired three Bell 47 helicopters for this purpose, and today boast approximately 225 aircraft mostly used for the offshore oil industry in the Gulf of Mexico.

In 1947, the Kerr-McGee company drilled the world's first commercial oil well out of sight of land in the Gulf of Mexico. As with lighthouses, the first service to offshore locations was conducted by boat. A regular helicopter service started in the late 1950s, and since then has only increased in volume to the numbers present today. The Gulf of Mexico, the Persian Gulf, the North Sea and many other offshore locations provide the main demand for helicopter services in the world.

The development of the oil rig helidecks outdates that of the lighthouse. Oil rigs are much larger structures and provide at least two options for the location of a helideck. The first is on top of the main buildings, preferably the higher ones. The second is a cantilever construction that positions the helideck away from the oil platform. Both constructions existed as early as the 1950s and ever since.

Alan Bristow, who pioneered a fifty-miles-long regular helicopter service to Doha in the Persian Gulf, documented the problems involved with one of the first helicopter services to offshore oil rigs. He states: 'The flight deck which was built on a cantilever structure attached to one side of the drilling rig, measured 50×70 ft. over all, and was raised some 60 ft. above the sea.' In addition he remarks that 'Weather records showed that 50% of the year the swell and sea was such in the drilling area that marine craft could not come alongside the rig to transfer personnel and equipment.' Already at that time he remarks that his passengers 'were to use the helicopter like a bus service'.[Bristow 1956:5-7]

Protection from the rough seas and speedy transport are the overriding reasons for helicopter services in the oil and gas industry as well as the necessary installation of helidecks. The size of these helidecks and today's safety regulations concerning their construction put the top-of-the-lantern platforms in a different light. When studying, for instance, the Norsok Standard c-004 published by the Norwegian Technology Centre on 1 November 2002, with regard to its North Sea platforms, it appears that the size of the lantern deck, the access to fire equipment, and the escape routes do not meet the standards of the oil industry. The Joint Aviation Requirements that are being introduced

Oil rig at location K8-FA-1
(Photo: courtesy of NAM)
← Oil rig at location L15
(Photo: courtesy of NAM)

throughout Europe have been forced to make an exception for lighthouse heli-decks, since they do not meet the safety requirements and they are not likely to meet these requirements at a later date.

The platform BID Dowsing in the service of Trinity House shows that oil plat-forms and lighthouses may share the same seas and facilities. The safety of personnel is better guarded by oil rig platforms allowing mass transport of people. Lighthouse helipads are not so much safe or suitable for transporting people; they are examples of engineering excellence on top of historic exam-ples of the same.

The oil rig helipads combine the safety measures designed for helidecks on ships and the structural possibilities for those on land. Both lighthouses and oil platforms still make use of ships, and nowadays nearly all supply ships and light vessels carry a helideck. The ships share a history with aircraft carriers. Ships and aircraft merged two generations earlier, and are part of the history of the ship's helideck.

— The ship

The combination of ship and aircraft was a military matter. The Royal Navy of Great Britain was the first to develop the thought during the First World War. The term aircraft carrier was used since 1916, but its development was ham-pered by navy and air force competition.[Robbins 2001:9] Seaplanes had been in use by the navy since 1914, but the development of aircraft carriers competed with air force interests. Similar delays frustrated the German, French and Italian attempts, and by 1939 only Japan and the United States had success-fully commissioned aircraft carriers. Robbins concludes: 'The Pacific campaign of the Second World War was the catalyst for the development of the carrier as the capital ship of the modern navy.'[Robbins 2001:10]

Just before the Second World War, the first helicopters became operational. Their combination with ships did not require a forty-year development. They were simply added to the aircraft carriers and to other navy ships with added platforms. They found their use in rescue missions, submarine hunts, and mine detection. The helideck was a simple addition to any ship; deck space was the only worry.

The ship's helideck is quite likely the first helicopter platform ever built. As soon as the American army and navy became convinced of the use of helicop-ters in its operations, they started training helicopter pilots on the merchant ship *Daghestan* in 1943.[NYT 1943a:21, NYT 1943b:29] It was fitted with a landing deck and it carried so-called 'Sikorsky HNS-1' helicopters. Trials on this 60×80 feet deck showed that the possibilities of the helicopter in submarine hunts were to be sought in coastal waters at least until models with improved performance would become available. On 29 June 1944, helicopter pioneer Frank Erickson landed on the deck of the ship *Cobb,* previously a coastal passenger vessel. This ship had been converted to a helicopter carrier; it was one of the first to deserve that name. The original potential for submarine hunts was overshadowed by the accomplishments in rescue missions. The same Erickson had made the fam-ous plasma flight to Sandy Hook on 2 May 1945. Later, eleven Canadians were rescued when marooned in Northern Labrador by the same US coast guard.

In 1952, the feasibility of helicopters as aerial minesweepers was demonstrated by the US Navy, and around 1960 the helicopters had self-sufficient minesweeping equipment for their operations. But, it was amphibious warfare and not minesweeping that transformed the ships to carry helicopters.

The Anglo-French operations off Port Said and Suez in 1956 revealed a weakness in Britain's organization for conducting amphibious warfare.Schofield 1969:296 As a result, the light fleet carrier *Bulwark* was converted to a so-called 'commando carrier'. In 1960, her fixed-wing capability had been removed, and alterations had been made to enable her to operate sixteen Westland Whirlwind helicopters as well as to carry a Royal Marine Commando of seven hundred and fifty men. In 1962, the HMS *Albion*, a sister ship of *Bulwark*, joined her after a similar conversion. The helicopter carrier had not replaced the aircraft carrier. It was mostly the smaller carriers that were converted to helicopter carriers for amphibious warfare.

The United States Navy initiated the conversion of fixed-wing aircraft carriers to helicopter carriers as early as 1948. The US Navy had adopted helicopters for amphibious warfare in July 1947, and they had subsequently decommissioned the observation squadrons on 5 April 1948. Fixed-wing aircraft were to be replaced by helicopters aboard battleships and cruisers by 30 June that same year. On 27 January 1949, the US Navy authorized the conversion of all newly-constructed cruisers to accommodate helicopters. see Van Vleet, Pearson & Van Wyen 1970

In peace time, the military helicopters frequented hospitals prior to the existence of ambulance helicopters and touched down anywhere they wished. The military did not need helipads apart from those on ships. They made full use of the helicopters' flexibility when it came to on-shore landing spots. Their port was the military airbase. Rooftop and island helipads have not been a military initiative. Instead, in times of disaster, the military helicopters are requested to conduct rescue operations from places where such facilities are missing. After the development of the aircraft carrier, the military developed attack helicopters and perfected search and rescue operations, especially landings on ships in high seas.

The Geneva Convention of 12 August 1949 (Article 35) protects the air ambulance from enemy attack, just in time for the various helicopter war rescue missions that followed in the 1950s. Unfortunately, it does not protect the air ambulance if it flies behind enemy lines, the area where the strong point of the helicopter is often found.

The Royal Dutch Navy

The Royal Dutch Navy acquired twenty-two Westland Lynx helicopters in the early 1980s. In 2005, one of these was lost, but all twenty-one remaining helicopters were still part of the organization. The operation budget allows fourteen of these to be in service, of which about five are operational at any one time. The helicopters are part of two squadrons of the Dutch Navy. Squadron 7 is responsible for search and rescue operations and Squadron 860 is the unit responsible for helicopters on board of navy vessels.

As of July 2004, the Royal Dutch Navy has boasted fifteen ships with helidecks. One amphibious transport ship or modern 'Bulwark', the *Hr Ms Rotterdam*, has a landing platform dock (LPD) for six medium-size helicopters. Two auxiliary or supply ships, *Hr Ms Zuiderkruis* and *Hr Ms Amsterdam*, have large plat-forms and a hangar that could house approximately two Lynx helicopters. Finally, four air-defence and commando frigates as well as eight M-class frig-ates also have smaller decks with hangar facilities for one helicopter. Heli-copters that are too large may transport supplies or people by way of a winch. Hovering above deck also allows for refuelling or HIFR (helicopter in-flight refuelling) via fuel lines leading from the helicopter to a fuel pump located in the deck surface.

All helidecks are placed aft and have hangar facilities. The Lynx helicopters can fold their rotors and hinge their tail to fit the space. The decks are cleared for landing by removing the fence-structure and folding it horizontally and out-wardly, providing space and safety netting for the helicopter and passengers. The grid in the centre of the deck accommodates a hook from the helicopter to secure the machine in place, after which the rest of the helicopter, particu-larly the rotors, may be secured to the deck with safety lines. The decks are specifically fitted for landings at (high) sea. Deck landings in the home port of Den Helder are not permitted, or occur by special permission only, for reasons of safety. The Lynx helicopters are to be replaced by the NH90 and discontin-ued completely in 2010. This new model helicopter is too heavy for landings on the M-class frigates, and will change the ratio of helidecks and helicopters.

In the Royal Dutch Navy, there are three times as many helidecks as there are operational navy helicopters. Similar to Dutch hospitals, helicopter platforms are landing opportunities rather than permanent stations. Deck operations and layout, the type of ships and the number of ships and helicopters differ per country and per year. On deck the difference is found with, for instance, American harpoon systems that land helicopters at high seas and Russian hangars that move across the deck to cover the helicopter. Large navies have also introduced aircraft carriers, only one of which was ever part of the Dutch Navy, with helicopters and airplanes, significantly increasing the number of helicopters in relation to helidecks.

In peacetime, the navy helicopters have excelled in rescue missions since the beginning of Dutch naval helicopter operations in the 1950s. But, even the navy is not exempt from prestigious transport. Geldhof mentions that the trans-port of VIPs by helicopters had become common place for the Dutch Royal Navy by 1968.[Geldhof 1987] VIPs and ships have enjoyed helicopters since the beginning. For instance, the Marine One has served the US presidency since 1947, and the FA-223 V12 helicopter was designated to rescue Benito Mussolini from his mountain prison in September 1943 but failed. Today, the Alouette III helicopters employed by the Royal Dutch Air Force are reserved for the trans-portation of the Dutch royal family. The explanation for helidecks on civilian decks is perhaps found in those prestigious tasks.

Civilian decks

The Korean War, starting in 1950, brought a large fleet of military helicopters into action. Aircraft carriers hosted helicopters, but apart from warships, the US Navy hospital ships, such as the *USS Consolation* and the *USS Repose,* also had a large aft helideck installed with a traditional red cross as the landing mark. The *USS Haven* hospital ship needed landing floats on either side of the ship to

Helidrome Architecture

HMS *Zuiderkruis*, Royal Dutch
Navy, Den Helder, The Netherlands

allow for landings of the same helicopters.[Ridgeway & Clark Report 1954:224, 282, 283] It was one of the first signs that ships other than battleships might benefit from helidecks.

Size, the kind that prohibits the use of aircraft carriers for private or commercial use, also limits civilian operations with ships and helicopters. Apart from helicopters on supply ships for the oil industry and the occasional vessel for the lighthouse board, commercial enterprises with ships and helicopters are largely absent.

Aristotle Onassis asked Alan Bristow, who pioneered oil rig helicopter services in the Persian Gulf in 1956 and delivered supplies to Wolf Rock lighthouse in 1948, for a whaling adventure.[Healey 2003:26–27] Onassis had a tanker refitted in 1950 for his Olympic Whaling Company, and had a large helicopter platform installed aft of the ship. Onassis' fortunes had benefited significantly from the trade boom induced by the Korean War.[Harlaftis 1996:264] Now, Onassis was planning to use a Hiller 360 helicopter for whale-spotting in the Antarctic. Bristow was sought after as an expert Hiller pilot. He set up Air Whaling Ltd and developed a special harpoon:[Rees 2003:52]

> This followed on from primitive tests in 1950, with a Portuguese company, when it was determined that more success could be obtained by striking the whale on the head with the nose wheel of the Westland-Sikorsky WS-51 being used for the trials!

By the time the harpoon and the right kind of helicopter had been recognized, the Whaling Commission of 1956 discouraged whale hunting altogether. The

Air Whaling adventure resulted in Bristow's appointment by Shell Oil's managing director of Shell Aircraft Ltd, Group Captain Douglas Bader, to provide the crew for their Persian Gulf service.

In 1995, Greenpeace used a helicopter to harass a Japanese whaling ship, and today, the Greenpeace fleet boasts large helidecks on the aft deck.[CNN 1998] Greenpeace enhanced its effectiveness by using helicopters as well as rubber boats, also known as zodiacs. The necessary helideck was proudly featured in one of their Dutch advertisement campaigns.[Metro 2003]

The fortunes of Onassis, the media attention sought by Greenpeace and the profits of the oil industry — their helidecks are closely connected to the prestige and wealth associated with helicopters in general. Still, the introduction of helidecks to luxury yachts and cruise ships, the epitome of prestige and wealth, has been a slow and a relatively recent development.

Yachts and ocean liners

Luxury yachts rarely reach the size that facilitates a helipad. Those that do, have little to gain from the small-scale helicopter service; the yacht itself overpowers the ostentation that a helicopter could possibly bring.

In 2001, the luxury yacht *Christina* was restored to its former glory with a 565 square feet helicopter deck. The yacht was originally owned by Aristotle Onassis, who, from 1954 until his death in 1975, made it his home. At that time, located above the smoking lounge, there was a flight deck that housed a seaplane. Onassis employed seaplane pilots, who made trips to the mainland.[Cafarakis 1971:24, 107, 186] They also used a landing area at his private island of Skorpios. When Aristotle Onassis bought the island of Skorpios in 1963, he had the top of the mountain cut off to make room for a helipad. On this private island, the seaplane apparently did not satisfy all his needs.

Later yachts of similar size were built for the Saudi Arabian royals, for instance.[Baker 2000:694] The *Al Yamana*, built by Elsinore SB&Eng. in Denmark, was intended for Saddam Hussein, who had named the ship *Qadissayat Saddam*. But Hussein gave it to King Fahd in 1987, after it had come into Iraqi service in 1981. The 2,282-ton yacht featured an aft helideck above the swimming pool. Helsingor Vaerft in Denmark delivered another royal yacht, the Abdul Aziz, to the Saudi royal family two years later. This ship, almost twice as long and three times as heavy, had a vehicle garage in addition to a swimming pool. A helicopter hangar and landing pad had been constructed forward, beneath the forecastle. It allowed the helicopter to be hidden rather than put on display in which case it would limit the view of the ship's captain.

Ocean liners, predecessors of the cruise ship, featured aircraft before they welcomed helicopters. The examples are not as prominent as those in the military context, but Miller notes the *Bremen* and the *Europe*.[Miller 1981:40] They were both built in 1929, and they successfully competed in the race for the fastest Atlantic crossing:

> Early in their careers a seaplane resting in a catapult was placed between the two funnels of each ship. Thirty-six hours before the ship docked the mails were sent ahead by air ... The scheme succeeded for a time, but in the end proved costly and awkward. By 1935, the technique was skipped.

Overview of yachts as discussed in the text

* Year in which ship started civilian operations
# Only the main purpose is stated: nearly all helidecks may also be used for medical emergencies.

Owner (Class)	Name (Type of ship)	Year* (built)	Tonnage/Wharf	Use of helipad #	Loc.
Aristotle Onassis	*Christina* (Private yacht)	1954	2,250 gt Howaldts Werke, Kiel, Germany	(seaplane)	upper
J.P. Papanicolaou	*Christina Onassis* (Yacht for hire)	2001	Victor Lenac, Croatia	personal transport	upper
Saudi Arabia	*Al Yamana*	(1981)	2,282 gt Elsinore SB, Denmark	personal transport	aft
	(Private yacht, navy patrol vessel)	1987			
	Abdul Aziz	1989		personal transport	fore
	(Private yacht, navy patrol vessel)				

As with luxury yachts, the helipad on an ocean liner is not the main attraction, although it does have a larger potential audience. This crowd is drawn to operations on ocean liners that invariably concern (medical) airlifts of passengers or crew. But, even the majestic *Queen Elizabeth II* of Cunard Cruiselines, which was commissioned in 1964, did not feature a helipad until it was requisitioned for the Falklands war in 1982, and was fitted with three of these between 3 May 1982 and 12 May of the same year:Butler 2003:397

> This latter task [creating landing areas for helicopters] involved actually cutting away some sections of the aft superstructure on the Upper and Quarter decks and covering the swimming pools with prefabricated steel decking to provide space for the helipads.

After this episode the Sun Deck featured as helicopter platform in case of emergency. Beneath the deck chairs yellow circles and a yellow H were visible, while the area itself was shielded with glass windscreens. Some preparation was required before a safe helicopter landing could be performed. The original steel helidecks were all removed after its war service had been completed.

The *Queen Mary II,* which was announced in 1998, became the then-largest passenger ship of the world in December 2003. Its thirteenth deck is a possible helicopter landing area. The teak deck and the deck chairs hide the yellow markings. The position of the upper decks of the QEII and QMII make their helidecks invisible from any standpoint unless the deck is cleared and approached from the air.

Icebreaker helidecks

The helideck has a different potential during (ant)arctic cruising, itself preceded by government vessels cruising the polar seas. The use of icebreakers and helicopters also goes back to Onassis when he sailed his whaling ships into polar waters. Lars-Eric Lindblad, a Swedish American, pioneered expedition cruises in the late 1960s, and he made his first voyage to Antarctica in 1966. Ward 2004:96 The use of icebreakers in the cruise industry entered a new era with the fall of the Soviet Union which then made (nuclear) icebreakers available for commercial purposes.

Icebreakers accommodate helicopters for ice reconnaissance as well as for cargo and passenger lifts. A hangar is desirable to protect the helicopters from

Operator	Name	Year	Tonnage/Wharf	Use of helipad	Loc.
Poseidon Arctic Voyages	*Yamal*	1992	23,445 gt	reconnaissance, excursions	aft
	(Nuclear icebreaker)		Baltic Shipyard & Engineering, Denmark		
Orient Cruise Lines	*Marco Polo*	1993 (refit)	22,080 gt		
	(Cruise ship with reinforced hull)		Knud Hansen, Denmark	medical, reconnaissance	upper
Murmansk Shipping Company	*Kapitan Khlebnikov*	(1981)	12,288 gt, Warsila Co, Finland	reconnaissance, excursions	aft
	(Icebreaker)	1994			
	Kapitan Dranitsyn	(1980)			
	(Icebreaker)	1994			

salt spray and its corrosive effects during long voyages. The passenger ice-breakers may also employ the machine for whale spotting. While ship-based helicopters have improved polar reconnaissance, they significantly increase the cost of an expedition.see MacDonald 1969:49, 163–167

In 1991, a ship formerly known as the *Alexandr Pushkin,* which had travelled between Montréal and Leningrad for the Russians, was sold to a Mr Herrod to become the first ship of his Orient Cruise Lines. Renamed *Marco Polo,* the twenty-five-year-old ship was completely overhauled by the Danish naval architect Knud Hansen, A&M Katzourakis interior designers, and the Neorian and Perama shipyards in Greece. Its tonnage had been increased from 19,860 to 22,080 tons, mostly for the increased passenger capacity of 826. The original ship had been built to navigate through broken ice. The strength of the hull was of much interest when in 1993 it initiated cruises to the Antarctic. With this purpose in mind, the ship had been fitted with a helipad on the top deck just behind the funnel. This deck stowed a helicopter during the Antarctic cruises to scout for whales, other marine life, and bad weather.

The 12,288-ton *Kapitan Khlebnikov* was built in Finland in 1981 by Warsila Company, one of the leading builders of icebreakers. Since 1994, it has taken passengers on board for (ant)artic cruises and has since been upgraded to accommodate more people. Its large aft helicopter deck may house two heli-copters for shore excursions. This ship allows a maximum of one hundred and twelve passengers, a number more appropriate for Antarctica where the IAATO — the International Association of Antarctica Tour Operators, founded in 1991 — has stated that no more than one hundred passengers should be brought on land at one time.

The *Kapitan Dranitsyn*, with a maximum of ninety-two guests but with equal tonnage, was built by the same Finnish company that produced another eight ships in this class. The *Dranitsyn* is mostly used in the arctic regions. Since 1994, it has carried passengers and can also accommodate two six-seat heli-copters. The ship is still owned by the Russian government, and it is also used for scientific expeditions. It was superseded by the *Yamal,* which breaks its trips all the way to the North Pole. This 23,445-ton nuclear icebreaker has

Helidrome Architecture

taken passengers since its completion in November 1992, with a maximum of one hundred at a time. It is one of four icebreakers of this class operated by Murmansk Shipping Company. Two helicopters can be found on board for reconnaissance and passenger excursions.see Ward 2004

Of the present thirty member ships of the IAATO and the few additional icebreakers operating only in the north, only four boast a helicopter on board, three of which are icebreakers. The remaining ships house a fleet of zodiacs that bring people ashore or show them around. Large cruise ships that have room for a helideck rarely transport their passengers by air. Smaller ships have little room for a helideck and in those distant waters mostly limit themselves to the use of rubber boats.

Today's visible cruise ship helidecks

Today, Star Cruises operates cruise ships in the Asia-Pacific region, and at least two of its ships, built in 1999, feature a helipad on the aft deck behind the funnel. Their thirteenth deck can only be observed from the top fourteenth deck and has a yellow circle eighteen metres in diameter, a yellow inner circle ten metres in diameter, and a capital H indicating its purpose. The *Super Star Leo* and the *Super Star Virgo*, both 76,800 tons and allowing a maximum of 1,960 passengers, have this feature on a spacious deck that still leaves room for manoeuvring. The location and the frugal advertising that this helideck receives have not made it into a prestige feature.

The helideck on cruise ships has been given a larger audience with the introduction of the Eagle Class by Royal Caribbean Cruiselines in 1999. The *Voyager of the Seas* built by Kvaerner Masa-Yards is the largest of the cruise line, though slightly smaller than the *QMII*, with an overall length of 311 metres and 137,268 tons, and features a round observation and helicopter deck at the tip of the bow. The video *Voyager of the Seas: building the world's largest cruise ship* presents the helideck as a first in the cruise industry. Its producer and director Fred Ashman mentions the controversy concerning the helideck within the cruise industry.Ashman 2004, pers. comm. It is emphatically stated that the pad is not to be used for passenger excursions. Its location — on other ships known as the rope or winch deck, accessible to crew only — is visible and accessible to passengers. The green-coloured platform with yellow markings is accentuated with benches that follow the rounding of the outer yellow circle. The pad is used for the occasional aerobics classes or for a medical emergency airlift, at which time the benches, wisely, are removed. Four sister ships feature the same: *Explorer of the Seas* in 2000, *Adventure of the Seas* in 2001, *Navigator of the Seas* in 2002, and *Mariner of the Seas* in 2003, all built by Kvaerner Masa-Yards in Finland. In 2001, a second class had been developed with a similar design.

The *Radiance of the Seas*, completed in 2001, was the first ship of Royal Caribbean Cruiselines with a helicopter deck that no longer featured as an observation or sun deck. The deck clearly signals that a helicopter is welcome at any time, although strings of decorative flags can be in the way. Shore excursions in Alaska, one of many places where Royal Caribbean sends its ships, feature heli-hiking and helicopter sight-seeing, but passengers take buses to a heliport from which to depart. Again the helideck is only meant for emergency

Overview of cruise and ferry lines as discussed in the text

* Year in which helipads were added during military operations, several refits in later years.

Cruise line	Name	Year	Tonnage/Wharf	Use of helipad	Location
Cunard Cruiselines	*Queen Elizabeth II* (Ocean Liner)	1969	70,327 gt, Upper Clyde		upper
		1982 (*)	Shipbuilders, Great Britain		
	Queen Mary II (Cruise ship)	2004	150,000 gt, Chantier de l'Atlantique, France	medical, sun deck	upper
Star Cruises	*Super Star Leo* (Cruise ship)	1998	75,338 gt, Meyer Werft,	medical	upper
	Super Star Virgo (Cruise ship)	1999	Germany		
Royal Caribbean	*Voyager of the Seas* (Cruise ship)	1999	137,268 gt, Kvaerner,	medical, observation deck	bow
Cruiselines	*Explorer o.t. Seas* (Cruise ship)	2000	Masa-Yards, Finland		
(Eagle class)	*Adventure o.t. Seas* (Cruise ship)	2001			
	Navigator o.t. Seas (Cruise ship)	2002			
	Mariner o.t. Seas (Cruise ship)	2003			
Celebrity Cruises	*Millennium* (Cruise ship)	2000	90,228 gt-91,000 gt,	medical	bow
(Millennium class)	*Infinity* (Cruise ship)	2001	Chantier de l'Atlantique,		
	Summit (Cruise ship)	2001	France		
	Constellation (Cruise ship)	2002			
Minoan Lines	*Knossos Palace* (Passenger Ferry)	2000	37,482 gt-37,000 gt,	medical (?)	aft
	Festos Palace (Passenger Ferry)	2001	Fincantieri, Genoa, Italy		
	Olympia Palace (Passenger Ferry)	2001			
	Europa Palace (Passenger Ferry)	2002			
Royal Caribbean	*Radiance o.t. Seas* (Cruise ship)	2001	90,090 gt, Meyer Werft,	medical	bow
Cruiselines	*Brilliance o.t. Seas* (Cruise ship)	2002	Germany		
(Radiance class)	*Serenade o.t. Seas* (Cruise ship)	2003			
	Jewel of the Seas (Cruise ship)	2004			

airlifts of the occasional patient whose open view of the landing spot perhaps sooths the earlier apprehension of being trapped on or winched from a ship. Three more ships of the Radiance class have appeared so far. The *Brilliance of the Seas* in 2002, the *Serenade of the Seas* in 2003, and the *Jewel of the Seas* in 2004 were all built by Meyer Werft (Jos L. Meyer) in Papenburg, Germany. Royal Caribbean Cruiselines and Celebrity Cruises merged in 1997. Celebrity Cruises brought its own *Millennium* class ships in 2000, built by Chantier de l'Atlantique in France. It was followed by *Infinity* in February 2001, *Summit* in September 2001, and *Constellation* in May 2002.[Celebrity Cruises Press Office 2002] Each features a helideck on the bow of the ship. This time the helicopter feature is neither advertised nor even mentioned on deck layouts in their brochures or on their website. Royal Caribbean and Celebrity do not mention the helipads in their press releases, in which they take pride in all the other new or remarkable features on board. Since their helideck is exclusively used for medical emergencies, it is not a main attraction. The association of wealth with helipads is lost on their marketing managers.

So far, cruise ships and icebreakers have used helipads for medical and reconnaissance purposes. In 2000, Minoan Lines proudly presented their newest

Helidrome Architecture

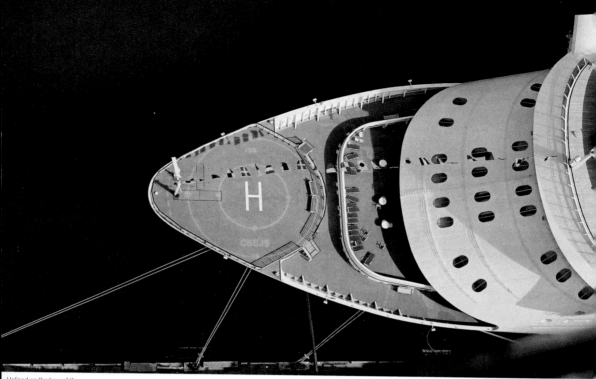

Helipad on the bow of the
Brilliance of the Seas, Royal
Caribbean Cruiselines, Miami,
USA

ferry, *Knossos Palace*, to service the route from Piraeus to Crete (Heraklion). It is the first of a series of four ordered from the Italian wharf Fincantieri in Genoa. Above a maximum of three hundred and ten cars or sixty-two trailers per deck and nearly five hundred passengers, it boasts a large helideck located aft behind the funnel. The ferry is meant to be fast and luxurious. The helideck has served to bring some dignitaries on board when the ship was chartered for an international conference; any other purpose has not been made explicit. But, with a ferry crossing of six hours from Piraeus to Heraklion, the helideck is hardly servicing remote locations.

Ships of the Royal Dutch Navy are not allowed to make helideck landings in port; they service their war ships at sea only. Cruise ships operate in an opposite manner. Royal Caribbean cruise ships are more likely to make landings in port or at least coastal waters rather than at high seas due to the more volatile pitching movements of a ship's bow. The absence of equipment and flight deck officers also prevents a safe operation of such landings. As with most hospital ships with a helideck, cruise ships and the occasional ferry operate their helipad for medical emergencies and without the permanent presence of helicopters. The navy ships and icebreakers that carry helicopters use the helideck as a permanent base from which reconnaissance flights, excursions and medical evacuations take place. Contrary to lighthouse and oilrig helipads, the first purpose of the ship's helideck is different from carrying passengers back and forth to the mainland. There are too many passengers and too few helicopters compared to the size and number of helidecks.

Structural distinction of the ship's helideck

The ship's wooden upper deck has been used as a helipad without the special surface paint and structural reinforcements. The helidecks on war ships are reinforced structures placed on a ship with an occasional hangar. The latest cruise ships integrate the helideck on the fo'c's'le or behind the funnel aft on the upper deck, with the appropriate present-day deck surface. In all cases, the helideck is not much different from any other deck with a broad view.

When the ship is in motion, the cruise decks are rarely appropriate or safe, particularly when the helideck is placed on the bow. Even with decks located aft, specialist air marshals, deck hooks, and necessary pilot training make helideck landings on moving vessels a separate type of helicopter operation. In order to avoid the risk of a slippery helideck, additional nettings on the deck surface may be found to allow sufficient grip for the helicopter undercarriage. Offshore industry and navy operations are alone in pursuing these possibilities. Their exercises at sea also make a hangar more appropriate. Hangars have forced helicopters to fold while some Russian hangars fold open to house helicopters still on deck.

The icebreakers mix navy operations with cruise vacations. They carry helicopters and sometimes feature hangars; they allow landings at sea but usually in tranquil polar waters; and they move passengers as well as scout the environment. The helideck is located aft, so far the preferred location for most helideck operators.

The helideck competes with other amenities on deck so that, for instance, lower decks take over the rope or winch function for anchors and shore lines. The mid-ship location behind the funnel competes with tennis courts and sun decks on cruise ships, but is generally less preferred since the turbulence caused by the location and the heat of the funnel are to be avoided. Otherwise, the sea provides a clear and unobstructed flight path.

— Shifting purpose

Helicopters are particularly apt to service remote locations. The presence and use of helicopters indicate that helidecks are often more numerous than helicopters with the exception of the offshore oil and gas industry.

The lighthouse helipad was introduced for the safety of the keepers. The automation process reduced the use of helipads to the transport of maintenance personnel. The last helipad that was completed on top of a lantern served the keepers for less than a year. Its completion merely served their maintenance personnel.

The helideck is a prominent feature on navy ships but funds and material determine whether helicopters are stationed permanently. Most navy ships feature hangars and their use of helicopters at sea is found in reconnaissance or submarine hunts. While their purpose is clear, their presence is limited.

Icebreakers and whalers use helicopters for reconnaissance, just like the military. Their use appears to have little prestige attached to it. Cruise ships have featured helipads occasionally to facilitate medical airlifts. Helidecks have become more frequent on recent cruise ships. But, they are not considered, by cruise company or passengers, as a sign of wealth, prestige or ostentation.

Brilliance of the Seas, Royal
Caribbean Cruiselines, Miami,
USA

Royal yachts sometimes feature helipads. Yet, the helicopter, often permanently stationed, is only one of many ostentatious features, and plays a secondary role in the wealthy appearance of the ship.

Mountains prevent seaplanes and sea-going vessels from providing alternative transport. Some scaffolding or a set of co-ordinates suffice to create a helipad on these high-up locations, so that even heli-skiing is only associated with the wealth of helicopters and not with the engineered helipad.

The most prominent use of helicopters is found in the transport of oilrig workers from the coast to the offshore platform and back. Millions of flight movements, invisible to the gasoline consuming public, have given helicopters its first convincing scheduled transport service. In this case, even the helicopter does not add prestige to their operations.

When dignitaries are hoisted to a navy vessel and when ferries boast a helipad on their top deck, the purpose and appearance of helidecks shift back to needless ostentation. Some cruise ships turn their helideck into observation decks and even claim to be the first with such a facility in a bid for prestige.

Lighthouses with helipads are far removed from the coast and not easily observed by tourists, but postage stamps have given even those lighthouses a claim to fame, and their crowning helipads feature prominently on the pictures taken from above.

The helidecks and helipads modify their purpose and also their image in the course of time. Helicopter operations determine the prestige of the helipad while the helipad itself contributes little but a welcoming stage. Seaplanes, boats or zodiacs can also maintain transport services, and each may have a similar claim to prestige, wealth and exotic locations. The helipad merely adds a feat of engineering and the helicopter a safer mode of transport.

Helipads have become part of an architect's oeuvre. In an examination of hotels, villas, offices and skyscrapers, prestige surfaces as a possible reason for adding helipads. For a similar reason, a platform may be placed on top of a roof, where it becomes more widely visible.

— Hotel and house pads

Hotels

Great Britain has approximately 220 registered helipads, excluding those on hospitals. In 1996, more than sixty per cent of these, 135 to be exact, were located at country hotels.[Frost 1996] The helicopter landing zones are for the benefit of the guests. This large number of hotel helipads is not found in, for instance, the greater São Paulo area, Florida, Switzerland, or the Netherlands. It appears mostly a British feature.

It is possible to associate helicopters and country hotels with upper class, prestige, wealth, or even ostentation. For those who do, it brings an ideal opportunity to show that the helipad itself hardly adds to such an image. All British helipads at hotels appear located on ground level. Only twelve have a hard surface, commonly marked with an H. Of the 123 lawns that are used for this purpose, some 91 lawns are not marked in any way. Three heligrounds double as croquet lawns, six as golf courses, and one is a golf bunker. Of all grass and hard-surface helipads, less than ten feature a permanent eye-catching windsock.

The hotel helipad in Britain is a welcoming feature, but it is only the arrival of the helicopter that can draw attention.

Bangkok lists about a dozen helipads on hotels, which allow efficient transportation to Bangkok's international airport. In January 2006, the helicopter company Si-Chang Flying Service that serviced these hotels ceased the operations for airport transfers. It signed a contract with a television news company instead. The Bangkok hotel helipads are now in disuse. The Shangri-La Hotel has had a helipad since 1986 and the Grand Hyatt since the early 1990s. The Hilton Hotel completed its current building in 1997 with a helipad. In this case, the helipad has always been meant for emergencies only. The Hilton Hotel added a rooftop restaurant in 2006 that partly blocks the helicopter access routes. The Royal Orchid Sheraton Hotel, at the Charoen Krung Road, used the pad on top of the neighbouring River City shopping centre to allow airport transfers. The shopping mall has now surrounded the platform with sculptures of one of its art dealers, and features a small bar in the shape of a teahouse in the middle of the yellow markings. The helipad-bar enjoys the view of the river and of the former access route of helicopters.

The Bangkok hotels feature the helicopter service to the airport in their brochures, and in some cases constructed a platform visible to their guests. Most of these helipads are now waiting in vain to attract both man and machine.

São Paulo and to a lesser extent Rio de Janeiro in Brazil feature many hotels with helipads. They are not merely part of an airport service. Helicopters have access to so many buildings in the greater São Paulo area that they function as a private limousine service to any part of town. João Armentano built the Blue Tree Hotel in 2001. With two landings per day, its helipad is used relatively

Hotel Mélia, São Paulo, Brazil

▸ Blue Tree Hotel, São Paulo, Brazil

↗↑ View from the River City shopping

centre helipad on the Hilton rooftop

restaurant across the river, Bangkok,

Thailand

often by its guests. Hotel Meliá is located near the World Trade Center, and the helipad is used almost every other day, not so much by the hotel guests but by neighbouring businesses. Construtora OAS ltd, a large engineering and building firm with its head office in São Paulo, was responsible for its construction. Koningberger Vannucchi Associated Architects, located in São Paulo, built the facility for the Holiday Inn Suites that features a round helicopter platform overarching the rectangular roof. Finished in 2003 and with an average of one guest using the platform every day (for a fee) so far, the platform fulfils an occasional need. These hotels are just examples of São Paulo hotels featuring a helipad. Their network is not limited to hotels and airports, but is part of a city that is almost saturated with helicopter landing facilities.

Resorts

Luxury resorts on distant tropical islands need transport services for their affluent guests. Although helicopters seem an obvious choice, they have much competition from seaplanes.

The military used seaplanes, also referred to as floatplanes, as early as 1914. The occasional seaplane serves remote locations and sea-going vessels well enough without requiring the more expensive helicopter. Longer distances are commonly flown by seaplanes and not by helicopters. Rarely do seaplanes and helicopters compete. It would require a middle-distance remote location where airstrips are unavailable and the seas smooth enough to land both seaplanes in the water and helicopters on land.

The Maldives feature such locations. The Maldivian tourist industry ships people to remote locations, commonly luxury beach resorts, on a considerable scale. It prefers seaplanes to helicopters. The world's largest seaplane fleet operating from one base is located at Malé International Airport. Helicopter operations were in place for a limited time. The additional expense was moderate. Their main benefit was during nighttime and rough weather, something for which the seaplanes were unsuitable. Trials resulted in two helicopter crashes after which helicopter operations ceased altogether. Rough seas prohibit seaplane operations, but rough weather and night operations were not safe enough to keep helicopter operations in place. Safety concerns banned the helicopter from the Maldives, at least for the present. The neighbouring Seychelles harbour helicopters instead of seaplanes, and serve a similar tourist population travelling to equally remote atolls — safely.

The earliest photographs of Igor Sikorsky flying a helicopter include examples of helicopters with floats.[Delear 1969:191] It is difficult to conceive of a location where helicopters are not able to land and the water is a superior surface for touch downs. Floats significantly inhibit the helicopter's performance; they increase its drag and weight. Inflatables replaced most fixed floats once they became available, since floats are used mainly as emergency precautions for unavoidable landings on water. They are required particularly during long flights over water — such as the ones to oilrigs and lighthouses, the same operations that featured helicopters with floats in former days. Fixed floats, apart from training water landings, are a rare necessity. A start-up on water, which may swing the entire helicopter around its axis a few times before full control is gained of the machine, is as uncommon as a location for which a marine

House with helipad, Miami harbour, USA

helicopter is the only effective mode of transportation. Indeed, a pier that docks the seaplane already serves adequately as a helideck.

Houses

The ostentatious private ownership of a helicopter took off when helicopters became cheap. The mass-produced examples by Robinson Helicopters, introducing the $40,000 R22 in 1979 and delivering a record 310 of those per year in 1989 for the price of ±$100,000, reduced the helicopter to an expensive car both in size and expense. Privately owned helicopters may have existed since the early years, but the market for such helicopters did not develop much until the 1990s.

Any remote estate may reserve a piece of farmland for the purpose of helicopter landings. The government requirements are simple or almost non-existent and the helipad is nearly invisible. The helicopter itself is the possible embodiment of ostentation rather than the landing zone. Occasionally, examples of house-bound helipads in urban environments are found; indeed, Robinson Helicopters is offering an inexpensive lightweight helipad of less than 6.5×6.5 metres for this purpose. Again the lawn is also an option or an elevated structure in the backyard. A villa that accommodates a helicopter should at least have a sizable backyard for that purpose. Unlike deck space on a yacht, roof space on a house comes relatively cheap. It requires a flat roof, but other than the occasional chimney, there is little obstruction.

One such household helipad in Belvedère, Belo Horizonte, Brazil, shows a Robinson 44 Raven parked on top of a small building.[Abreu 2005] This modest structure houses relaxation facilities for those using the swimming pool or the neighbouring tennis court. The helipad does not have any of the official markings, and the location has a broad view and flight path over the Belvedère suburb. The view from the helipad also shows a lawn with the ground-based

helipad of the neighbours. The machine and its parking spot blend in with the overall luxuries of the villa and the neighbourhood.

The Brazilian architect Carlos Alexandre Dumont designed the above house in around 2002. The role of the architect in relation to helipads is more pronounced in the centre of the city. The camouflaged facilities of the suburban villa are only an introduction to the full view of the helipad mid-town, where the association with wealth can be equally obvious, but where the location is less protected from the pedestrian masses. In the city, it is not the helicopter but the platform and possibly its architect that may draw most of the attention.

— High-rising concerns

The congestion of the world's metropoles with high-rise buildings has not crowded them with rooftop helipads. Few examples exist where cities enjoy numerous helipads besides those on hospitals and police stations, but the few cities that do have record numbers. Helipad density is city-specific, often aided by generous regional and national regulations.

In April 1951, a rooftop heliport was in use on the top of the Port Authority sixteen-storey office building in New York.[NYT 1951a:38, 1951b:25] The roof service was established for officials of the Port Authority:[Law 1957:15]

> A 40×45 feet platform is used, set on steel columns attached to the existing building columns and raised 7 ft. above the roof ... Experience has proved beyond doubt that the use of helicopters for executive trips saves a great amount of valuable time.

It became the first high-rise helipad and the first for the purpose of transporting executives. New York has become only a modest helipad city, but has pioneered many civil helicopter enterprises. In later years, the high-rise executives would scour and devour the roofs of São Paulo and Los Angeles instead. São Paulo and Los Angeles are the most helipadded cities in the world. Brown describes city ordinances of the 1970s that could explain this circumstance. [Brown 1981:93] In 1972, a great fire in the Andraus building in São Paulo broke out and 450 people were rescued by eleven helicopters from its roof helipad. In 1973, the forty-storey Avianca building in Bogotá had 500 people rescued from its roof during a fire, which was originally detected by a traffic patrol helicopter. In 1974, another fire, this time at the Joelma building in São Paulo, saw one hundred people rescued by helicopter without the help of a platform. As a result, São Paulo and Los Angeles, where the news had made headlines, required rooftop landing zones for tall buildings, 35 meters and 24 meters respectively, as early as 1974. Chicago followed and required a rooftop clear zone for tall buildings in 1975.

This historical information provided by Brown is unknown to most Paulistas, inhabitants of São Paulo, and difficult to trace in today's regulations. The Ministry of Aviation in Brazil does not stipulate a helicopter platform, but an emergency landing zone for buildings over five stories high:

> [9.6.1] Mediante autorização do Comandante do Comando Aéreo Regional onde está localizado e com a finalidade de prever a evacuação dos ocupan-

Fitness room with helipad, Belvedère, Belo Horizonte, Brazil

From: Instruções para Operação de Helicópteros para Construção e Utilização de Helipontos ou Heliportos by Ministerio da Aeronáutica, Comando Geral de Apoio Diretoria e Eletrônica e Proteção o Vôo, Portaria no. 18/ M5, February 14, 1974 including amendments up o July 1983.

* Chapter 15 of the California Fire Code and Uniform Fire Code 'California ire Code', 1998 Edition, ompiled by the California Building Standards Comission and the 'Uniform ire Code', 1997 Edition, ompiled by the International Fire Code Institute nd the Western Fire Chiefs Association.

tes de edifícios em casos de incêndio ou outra calamidade, poderão ser construídas áreas de Pouso e Decolagem sobre edifícios com mais de 5 (cinco) pavimentos, após análise dos obstáculos constituídos por outros edifícios. *

In the case of the Dacon building, for instance, this type of landing zone was later converted into a helipad. The regulations governing the building and the use that is made of helipads partly explain the omnipresence of helipads in São Paulo today.

An ordinance of similar content is active in Los Angeles, it reads:
[Sec. 15-1-902.5.2] High-Rise Emergency Helicopter Landing Facility. Every high-rise building shall have an emergency helicopter landing facility located on the roof in an area approved by the Chief. The roof structure shall be designed and constructed to support a minimum live load of ten thousand (10,000) pounds (4536 kg). Such landing facility shall be installed as required for Helistops in Article 24. [Amended by Ord. No. 3518, eff. 06/26/99; 3424] **

In 1973, prior to the fire code regulations, Melville Branch published a study on urban air traffic, and provided a detailed overview of helipads in the greater Los Angeles area. He states that 'Metropolitan Los Angeles probably has today a more intensive peace-time use of helicopters than any other place in the world'.Branch 1973:xv He counts 175 helistops and heliports in the county of Los Angeles, with 63 for the city of Los Angeles. It appears that Los Angeles helipads were numerous prior to any fire.

Branch states that 'Aircraft landing facilities, including helistops and heliports, are permitted as a right in the "light" and "heavy" industrial zones.' In addition, the Fire Department is allowed to issue special helicopter permissions, allowing landing zones with less than three landings per day.Branch 1973:5,7 This leads to an increase in frequency and a decrease in justifications for special helicopter approvals. City, county, state and aviation authorities have influence in the recording and approval process, but in the absence of strict regulations the number of helicopter sites is likely to increase.

Fire departments and the federal aviation authorities approve helipads on the basis of safety for pilot, passenger, and building. Local governments are concerned with urban planning, noise abatement, and other political motivations. In Los Angeles, these latter concerns appear to have been set aside. Branch addresses these issues at length, and he states that:Branch 1973:39

> California recently passed legislation regulating heliports and helistops,
> but with so many exemptions and no inspection except in response to
> specific complaints, that it is mainly a licensing act.

The ground and rooftop helipads recorded by Branch are distributed evenly. Of the 62 helipads in the city that were recorded in 1971, 29 were installed on rooftops versus 33 on the ground. Rooftops included five government buildings, three police departments, two fire stations and one children's hospital. The public services were well represented. The remainder was part of highrises of the oil, banking, insurance, broadcasting and other industries including two hotels. Only two were part of helicopter service organizations. The ground-based platforms hardly differed in distribution, apart from having five aircraft industries and a few more police and fire departments with no ground pads for hospitals. By 1971, most if not all kinds of operations had found their way to the roof.

Branch suggests 'prestige' as an explanatory factor for the presence of rooftop helipads. He states:Branch 1973:40

> Developers of high-rise office buildings want helistops because they believe
> they add prestige, and they prefer them on the roof because of the high cost of
> land in the urban areas where such buildings are feasible. Air accessibility
> is the most important consideration in the design of the helicopter facilities,
> and air-taxi operators urge that their experience be taken into account in
> designing heliports and helistops, especially those on rooftops.

As always, government and hospitals disguise any ostentation of their platform under the cover of transport needs for the public good. Remote helipads also distance themselves from prestigious appearances. Rooftop helipads on any other building cannot hide behind public need but represent industry and wealth, at least in the eyes of Branch.

Today, Los Angeles shows helipads on nearly every high-rise building, but most of these landing zones are only to be used in case of emergency. Most helipads are invisible from the ground, apart from the occasional windsock. This situa-

Tallest buildings of Los Angeles in 2004

*   Height of the building is also the height of the helipad on the building.

**   Leading architect

Rank	Name(s) and address	Architect	Height*	Year
1	US Bank Tower; First Interstate World Center; Library Tower 633 West Fifth Street	Pei Cobb Freed & Partners (** I.M. Pei)	310 m	1990
2	AON Center; First Interstate Tower, 555 West Fifth Street	The Luckman Partnership, Inc.	262 m	1973
3	Two California Plaza, 350 South Grand Avenue	Arthur Erickson Architectural Corporation	229 m	1992
4	Gas Company Tower; SoCal Gas Center, 707 Wilshire Boulevard	Skidmore, Owings & Merrill LLP (** R. Keating)	228 m	1991
5	ARCO Center; BP Plaza; Security Pacific Bank Building, 333 South Hope Street	AC Martin Partners, Inc.	224 m	1974

tion has not given helipads additional status, since each tall building is provided with an example. For instance, four balconied apartment blocks, located between South Olive Street and South Hill Street at Second Street in downtown Los Angeles, each feature a helipad with permanent windsock and with lighting at night. Even if the residents intended to use a helipad, they do not require four of these. Since the most luxurious housing of Los Angeles is not found in this part of town, prestige is not likely to be attached to this amendment to the roof.

The US Bank Tower, better known as the Library Tower, is the tallest building in Los Angeles. It is also the tallest building in the world with a helipad. The AON Center was struck by the largest high-rise fire of Los Angeles on 4 May 1988. At that point it was still the tallest building in the city. The twelfth floor was on fire, five floors were destroyed, and one human life lost. A number of rescue workers were saved by helicopter from the helipad on top of the building, justifying the Los Angeles fire code.

The mandatory installation of helipads in the Los Angeles area has not encouraged architectural novelty in terms of construction. The California Bank Trust building at 550 Hope Terrace/South Hope Street is one of few exceptions where the helipad has become a prominent structural feature of the building. At 107 metres, it only ranks forty-eighth on the list of tallest buildings in Los Angeles. The cantilever support structure of the pad — designed by Kohn Pedersen Fox Associates, and completed in 1991 — is visible from the ground. It has become an integral part of the building rather than an add-on, such as antennas or air conditioning units on neighbouring buildings.

In contrast, the city of São Paulo does not feature mandatory helipads, but still has 220 helipads in the built-up city area. In this city, architects have expanded their role in the design of the helipad.

The São Paulo helipads

The turbine-engine Bell 206B Jetranger II was the first successful executive helicopter, but by the time of its introduction in 1966 and improvements to it in the 1970s 'the two most important decades of its [Brazil's] architectural

Dacon building prior to the conversion of the emergency platform to a helipad, São Paulo, Brazil
(Photo: courtesy of Ricardo Julião)
→ Dacon building with helipad São Paulo, Brazil
← Los Angeles skyscrapers
Left: Library Tower
Right: Gas Company Tower
↓ Los Angeles apartment buildings with helipads

development' had long passed.[Giedion 1956:x] The architects involved in Brazilian helipads are not the well-known Le Corbusier and Oscar Niemeyer. Their names are Carlos Bratke, Ruy Ohtake, and a long list of mostly São Paulo trained and raised architects whose claim to fame is found in the 1990s. In these later years, São Paulo has become known for its many helipads and its continuous construction boom. Although it does not have more helipads than Los Angeles, the helipads are located much closer together. The flight movements are less than those in New York, but they include business flights within the city as opposed to just sightseeing and commuter flights around Manhattan.

The local São Paulo helipad guide *Pilot's Help*, founded in 1999, lists most if not all helipads in the city, and provides aerial photographs so that the helipad's visibility to both pilot and pedestrian can be studied. The *Pilot's Help* of 2003 is used here to provide the first statistics, and, with over 200 listed helipads in the city of São Paulo, its estimates allow a first impression on the design of helipads in a city area.

For reasons of convenience, the number of high-rise buildings in the São Paulo area is estimated at 2,360. This number has been adjusted from the 2,872, which includes buildings under construction, on hold, or just approved or proposed.[see Emporis 2004] The 2003 *Pilot's Help* counts 236 helicopter platforms for the greater city of São Paulo, which, conveniently, shows that ten per cent of the high-rise buildings may have a helipad. This number, 236, includes low-rise buildings and ground-based helipads at hangars. In total, the city of São Paulo has put helipads on rooftops in not more than five per cent of the high-rise buildings.

This simplified statistic illustrates that the law stating a helipad is required on each building above 35 or even 80 meters (the cut-off point for the Emporis Data Committee) is not enforced.[Emporis 2004] Also, not every high-rise building owner desires a helipad or feels obliged to have one.

The data provided by *Pilot's Help* are incomplete. Thirty-two helipads, two of which are hospitals, are not accompanied by a photograph. Others are not part of high-rises. For instance, thirty-four helipads are based on the ground and two others have taken the shape of an independent structure. One of these is a raised platform in a backyard of a large house, the other is near a bus station. Twenty helipads are found on hospitals, and if these are excluded as well, one hundred fifty helipads remain.

About 83 helipads are clearly visible from the street, almost forty per cent of the grand total of 236 or about fifty-five per cent of 150. In two-thirds of the cases, these helipads are much broader than the roof, and are overhanging structures, immediately recognizable as helipads. The remainder is not larger but raised from the roof by means of a pedestal. This additional structure underneath the helipad is much smaller than the roof section, and it is often smaller than the size of the helipad.

Another fifty-four helipads cannot be seen from the street. The pad is smaller than the roof section, and has been placed at the same level or nearly the same level as the plane of the roof. Only a strategically placed windsock or an arriving or departing helicopter could betray the location.

This leaves thirteen examples, arguably some of the above examples are included as well, as neither visible nor invisible. In these cases, there is an

Helidrome Architecture

overhanging section, but not a visibly overhanging helipad. Some have a support structure on top of the roof, but without an overhanging helipad that is visible from the street. The architecture of the building has allowed for the *possibility* of a helipad.

Size of the helipad compared to the roof

The minimum size of a square helicopter platform in Brazil is 18×18 metres. This is large compared to the 9×9 metres used for lighthouses. The American and European regulations, mostly derived from the ICAO recommendations, indicate a minimum of 1.5 times the overall length of the helicopter. This allows most small and medium-size helicopters to land on a 12×12-metre helipad, including the air ambulances used in the Netherlands, Switzerland, and Brazil. Each Brazilian helipad shows a painted number on the platform, which indicates the maximum allowable weight in tons according to international regulations. Only five and six-ton helicopters occasionally need a larger than 18×18-metre platform. The largest helicopter in operation in the São Paulo area is the Sikorsky s76, which requires a 24×24-metre platform and a six-ton weight allowance. The 18×18 minimum appears an oversized rule.

The size of the landing spot is augmented by a corridor for passengers or fire men to safely pass around the helipad or by safety netting, which extends 1.5 metres from the platform to prevent people from falling off the roof. Safety zones around the landing spot extend three metres on all sides on the Dutch roof pads, and they often require additional netting as well. In Brazil, an average square platform is not smaller than 21×21 metres.^{see Neto 2006}

A high-rise building provides a commanding view over its surroundings, until new towers obstruct this view. While the view from the rooftop is much appreciated, the basic problem for the helipad is the roof size. Narrow roofs require a support structure that lifts the helipad above the roof and partly over the side. On low-rise buildings, this support structure may reach the ground, as does the Resgate helipad engineered by Carlos Freire. A tall building has a support structure fixed only to the roof, and has safety netting or concrete slabs sticking out from the roof for any pedestrian to admire.

Next to a sizeable platform, water reservoirs, antennas, air conditioning units, and other ventilation shafts compete for the available space, the view, and the fresh air. The structural answer to the roof competition is a division of the roof. The units are placed next to each other, if the roof is elongated enough, or above each other with a layer of fresh air supporting the helipad on the top layer. The cantilever helipad on oilrigs had the helipad hover above the sea; the helipad in São Paulo hovers above the roof, occasionally extending beyond its perimeters.

Hangars are not allowed on top of Brazilian roofs, and other equipment is not supposed to obstruct the flight paths of the helicopter. Only one hangar was constructed on top of a Brazilian building, and it needed a special structural solution; it was located inside the roof. In 2000, Brazilian architect Sérgio Assunção finished his Brigadeiro building. The helipad is recognizable from the street, but hidden from view depending on the direction from which the building is observed. The centre of the platform has a hatch that can open, and which features a hydraulic lift construction, designed and constructed by the Brazilian engineer Newton Nadruz. It transfers a small helicopter to the helideck or from the helideck into the building's hangar. It forms no obstruction to any flight path as long as the hatch is closed.

Size and the additional space needed for roof appliances contribute to the visibility of the Brazilian helipad.

— Skyscrapers' neutral contest

São Paulo's high-rise buildings do not exceed 170 metres, mostly due to the local building laws that prevent towering structures penetrating the approach routes to Congonhas airport nearby. High numbers pertain to the fleet of buildings over thirty-five metres, or twelve floors, which has made São Paulo, according to the definitions of the Emporis Data Committee, and after Hong Kong, New York City and Singapore, the city with the most skyscrapers. The highest of those with a helipad, Birmann 21, measures a mere 150 metres.

The race for the tallest building takes place in Asia. The race first initiated in the United States but moved east, although the United States are still a contender today. Status and prestige is strongly associated with the skyscraper, since its economic benefit, particularly above 150 metres, is doubtful while its symbolism remains strong.van Leeuwen 1986

Helipads above 150 metres are also not an economically interesting proposition. High-speed elevators outperform the helicopter in a race to the top, although its downward speed may be uncomfortably faster. The helipad does not even need the top spot for reasons of space or safety as the examples will show. The remote economic interest is flanked by the remote location of the top floor, taken to extremes when the helipad is raised two hundred metres or more. To be visible at the top, the windsock no longer draws attention from the crowds in the street. Extreme size or extraordinary constructions are necessary to make a helipad visible and noticeable that far up in the sky.

The competition

The all-time tallest building that featured a helipad was the WTC Twin Towers in New York. The helipad was placed on the top of the South Tower at just over 400 metres. It was invisible to the street audience, since the roof was large enough to hide this feature. In aviation terms, it is the height, that is, the metres above ground level, and not the elevation, that is the metres above mean sea level, that count. The scaffolding used by Hermann Geiger easily outperforms the Twin Towers in terms of elevation.

After the collapse of the towers, Los Angeles, the city with the most helipads, became also the city with the highest helipad found on top of the tallest building in Los Angeles: the US Bank Towers by I.M. Pei, formerly known as the Library Tower. As with the WTC, the helipad is hidden from view and located within its flat roof.

On the current ranking of tallest buildings in the world, this US Bank Tower ranks only twenty-first, with five much older buildings outsizing the construction. It indicates that, in contrast with the WTC in New York, the LA tower was never part of the race for the tallest building. The skyscrapers in Los Angeles simply follow the fire code, since the tallest buildings of Los Angeles all feature

Resgate (medical insurance company), São Paulo, Brazil
→ Brigadeiro building, São Paulo, Brazil
↑↑ The hatch of the helipad hangar on top of the Brigadeiro building
(Photo: courtesy of Newton Nadruz)

a helipad on their flat roof. An additional fourteen buildings in the world have passed the 310 metres of the US Bank Tower in Los Angeles since its construction in 1990, but only one of these features a helipad. This one building was to become the tallest hotel of the world.

The Burj Al Arab was commissioned to become the landmark building of the United Arab Emirates, more specifically Dubai. Building activities started in 1994, and were not completed until 1999. Situated on a man-made island 15 kilometres south of the city of Dubai, at 321 metres it is the tallest hotel building in the world. As a five-star hotel, it features suites, luxury suites, and presidential suites with pools and fountains, restaurants, and butlers.

Tom Watts at WS Atkins, an architectural company based in London, designed a transparent sail façade featuring a helicopter platform on the twenty-eighth floor, which measures twenty-four metres in diameter. The cantilever construction towers 211 metres above mean sea level, in this case equal to ground level, and can be seen protruding from the sail from most angles. It is opposite the Al Muntaha sky view restaurant, which also extends from the main building, overhanging the front side of the sail. Together, they accentuate the sail at crow's nest height.

A thirty-minute BBC documentary for Discovery Channel featured the Burj Al Arab as the 'World's most luxurious hotel'. Produced and directed by Mike Wiseman in 2002, the documentary includes an interview with Tom Watts, the building's architect, who characterizes the building with a simple drawing. His drawing includes two lines forming the sail and a little circle that indicates the helipad and restaurant. The documentary does not discuss, mention, or otherwise feature the helipad as opposed to the lobby, the Al Muntaha restaurant, the fountains, the window washers, and the falconer chasing the pigeons away. The window washers, falconer, and falcon have no use for the helipad.

Heli Dubai, a government owned helicopter company, was not operational until late 2004. It offers an airport–hotel service for the guests. The helicopter cuts travelling time from two hours down to approximately eight minutes. The high-density altitude of the helipad on hot days requires high-performance helicopters. Pilots need to be aware of significant updraughts and turbulence from surrounding structures. The helicopter company wishes to expand its helicopter service to interregional travel from the airport, but needs an improved helipad infrastructure within Dubai and its neighbouring countries.
Dawson 2005

The Dubai helipad is part of the characteristic architecture of the building, and attracts much attention from ground level. The documentary indicates that this attention shifts quickly once inside the building. The only information provided by the architects concerning the helipad is its height, 211 metres above ground. It did not reach the full height of the building, leaving the LA tower unopposed. The typical structure of the helipad had a sequel in Seoul.

At 165 metres, the Daewoo Electronics R&D Headquarters barely reaches the top twenty tallest buildings of Seoul. The ambition of the client, Daewoo Electronics, for this building was of another kind. Foster & Partners conceived it in 1995, and its erection is still in progress. It is nothing less than a landmark building for the city of Seoul. 'The profile of the skeletal form of this tapered slab tower has been likened to the hull of a traditional Korean ship, though in

Helidrome Architecture

View from the sky promenade of
the Midland Square building,
Nagoya, Japan

reality the shape optimizes the planning envelope regulations.'[Binder 2001:208]
The idiosyncratic cantilevered helipad that reinforces the sailing image had
no other place to go but out on a limb.

This time the helipad reaches the full height of the building. The open structure of the steel skeleton breathes air, and the cantilever construction leaves
extra room for the landing approach angles. The offices are inside the solid-core
concrete column, at walking distance from the helipad. Arrival by helicopter
on the open air platform adds a chilling walk along the top of the skeleton.

The Burj Al Arab does not feature the highest helipad, and its structure is no
longer unique either. Since it prides itself as the tallest hotel, it may well feature the highest helipad on a hotel. But in terms of hotels, the JR Central Towers
in Nagoya, Japan, have better numbers. Their office tower is 245 metres tall,
and the Nagoya Marriott Associa Hotel tower is 226 metres; both feature a helipad on the roof. Both platforms are slightly raised on a pedestal, making them
visible from a few angles on ground level. The sky lounge in either tower presents a view of the neighbouring helipad and in 2007, the 360 metres tall Midland Square nextdoor was completed with a prominent view of both helipads
from their sky promenade. The architects, Kohn Pedersen Fox Associates, do
not mention that they built the tallest hotel helipad in the world in 2000; it is
irrelevant.

Since the competition for the tallest building shifted to Asia in the 1990s, the tallest office, hotel and residential building have been located in Asia. Eight of the ten tallest buildings in the world are in Asia. If the tallest helipad is located in Los Angeles, at least the tallest helipad of Asia may seek some prestige from this feature.

In 2001, Hijjas Kasturi Associates developed the Menara Telekom Headquarters in Kuala Lumpur. Its 310 metres puts the total height at the same level as the US Bank Tower. The Telekom building takes the shape of a bamboo shoot. At approximately three-quarters of its height, it boasts a large round roof structure that supports a helipad. The helipad is forty metres in diameter, and 238 metres above ground level. The project director, Ahmad Shuheimi Bahaudin (2004), adds that the access route is via an emergency elevator that reaches Level 56. From that level, a tower escape staircase leads up to the flat roof on Level 59 that is connected to the helipad at Level 59 1/2 via an open metal staircase.[Bahaudin 2004, pers. comm.] As with all platforms on high-rise structures, the passenger access has not been the main concern of the architect. The round helipad of the Menara building is certainly meant to attract attention from the ground.

Three additional towers have been constructed next to the Menara Headquarters, and they all feature a large helipad on top of their roof. Contrary to downtown Kuala Lumpur, where the Petronas Towers dominate an area largely without helipads, the bamboo shoot allows new stems to create a helipad network on the outskirts of town.

The oversized, contrasting shape of the Menara tower stands out, and it at least suggests the presence of a helicopter platform. Although it reaches the same height as the LA tower, the helipad is located more than 70 metres lower, which makes this helipad higher than that of the Burj Al Arab, but not the highest in Asia.

The rooftop helipad on the 292-metre SEG Plaza in Shenzhen, China, is placed next to satellite antennas that overlook the city. Across town, only the Shun Hing Square building is taller, but lacks the roof pad to take its inhabitants further up. The helipad is level with the roof and invisible to the pedestrian eye. Unknowingly, indeed modestly, SEG Plaza has the highest helicopter landing platform in Asia, and since the collapse of the WTC Towers in New York, the second highest helipad in the world.

Hua Yi Designing Consultants, the architects, were not instructed by the SEG Plaza Investment & Development Company to build the tallest building, since four years earlier, in 1996, the Shun Hing Square had already given the city its pride with a building of 325 metres. The helipad, according to Binder, merely 'adds to the building's high-tech appearance'.[Binder 2001:166] The helipad is not part of a contest.

The eye-catching helicopter platforms on skyscrapers have not found their prestige in being the highest. The highest helipad on office and hotel, in Asia and the rest of the world, is consistently hidden from view.

The environment

The 1990s showed not only a race for the highest building in Asia, it also brought the 'green skyscraper' with energy conserving, peaceful qualities that would

The Nagoya Marriott Associa
Hotel, part of the JR Central
Towers, Nagoya, Japan
← Menara Telekom Head-
quarters, Kuala Lumpur,
Malaysia
Next page: The helipad and
balconies of the Menara
Telekom Headquarters

Overview world's highest helipads, 2004

* Height in metres above ground

Building	Architect(s), city, country	Year	City, country	Height* pad/roof
Highest hotel/building in 2004 with a helipad:				
Burj Al Arab	WS Atkins, London, UK	1999	Dubai, UAE	211/321
Highest elevated helipad construction on a hotel:				
JR Central Towers, Hotel	Kohn Pedersen Fox Associates, New York, USA	2000	Nagoya, Japan	226/226
Highest elevated helipad construction in Asia:				
SEG Plaza	Hua Yi Designing Consultants, Hong Kong	1999	Shenzhen, China	292/292
Highest elevated helipad construction in the world:				
US Bank Towers, Library Tower	I.M. Pei & Partners, New York, USA	1990	Los Angeles, USA	310/310
Highest elevated helipad construction in history:				
WTC Two	Emery Roth & Sons, New York, USA	1973–2001	New York, USA	415/415

enhance the well-being of the occupants. With this trend, the noise-polluting and fuel-guzzling helicopter may lose its possible popularity.

The green skyscraper is sensitive to ecological and environmental issues. Ken Yeang, a Malaysian-born architect, uses vegetation to regulate heat and purify air. He is sensitive to identity and regionalism in Southeast Asia, and incorporates all that is ecologically, environmentally and architecturally important to him in his building designs. The Shanghai Armory Tower is one of his latest works.[Powell 1999:92–95] It is an operationally energy-efficient building with landscaped sky-terraces that filter the air. The building is a circular tower, a 'symbolic interpretation of components found in military armaments'. The topmost extension of the building suggests a 'victorious torch', states Powell, when he points to the massive translucent round helicopter platform that hovers on slim legs above the roof. The building was designed in 1997 for the Pudong district of Shanghai, but is as yet unbuilt.

Ken Yeang confirms that the helicopter is not seen as unfriendly to the environment. As shown earlier, the machine has been used to hunt whales or to keep whalers from hunting. The Menara Telekom building shows gardens overhanging its balconies, suggesting an environmentally friendly building design despite its huge helipad. The Hankyu Chayamachi Building in Japan goes one step further. The harmless helicopter landing area is replaced by the useful helipad. It serves as a protection against the elements.

The Hankyu Chayamachi Building, also known as the Applause Tower, because of its second-floor theatre, houses the Hotel Hankyu International. It is just over 161 metres high, and is located in Osaka, Japan. This tall building has an active mass damper (AMD). This damper controls the movement of the building in response to high winds and earthquakes. With 480 tons, its rooftop helipad has been turned into the heaviest active mass damper in the world. It is placed on four dampers underneath the platform, while four actuators control the system. The Takenaka Corporation engineered the AMD in 1992, and pioneered a helipad that is a structural necessity to the design of a building.

— Shifting anticipation

The high-rise building is featured on film as often as the helicopter, but its helipad does not hold the same status. The possible prestige of the helipad is unrelated to that of helicopters, since the few ostentatious platforms in existence hardly show any flight movements.

The use of helipads on high-rise buildings is limited to landings of the occasional guest or the evacuation of the occupants. A large number of helipads on high-rise buildings can be found in Los Angeles and in São Paulo, but only in the latter city have architects integrated the helipads in the design of the overall building.

Outside these two cities, skyscrapers in other parts of the world occasionally feature a helipad. Their architects have changed the obvious location of the helipad. Structures halfway up the building or near the top floor resulted in just elevated rather than rooftop helipads.

In general, helicopter landings on high-rise buildings are rare. The architect who designs a helipad no longer envisions numerous flight movements — the transport idea dominant in early rooftop airport designs — but has turned the structure into a roof accessory.

Welcoming safety

Helipad height does not appear part of an international competition. Height merely introduces flying hazards. The height of the helipad makes low visibility flying conditions more frequent, since a low cloud base may sooner obstruct the view. The building itself increases the risk of turbulence, and on the top, the exposure to the elements is as dangerous as on a lighthouse. The surrounding city limits alternative landing zones. As a result, the top location seems the ultimate safety hazard. The dangers for pilot and aircraft have rightly limited high-rise rooftop landings to a minimum. However, most high-rise platforms are installed as a safety precaution to allow for roof evacuations.

The purpose of the skyscraper helipad is clouded not only by its distance from the ground, but also by the limited attention from reviewers and the scarce flight movements. It may not have any flight movements at all. Still, the helipad is not as superfluous as Robert Byron's balcony, even though the idle state of most helipads and their accessorily attachment to buildings strike a resemblance:[Byron 1928:113–114]

> In both inner and outer London ... it is *vulgar* to sit upon a balcony ... Nor are provincial towns less squeamish. And in the country the balcony is superfluous, Either the sun shines, when we rush into the garden to see it. Or else it does not, when we stay indoors. The balcony, in fact, remains the instrument only of suicides. Each one is a lasting memorial to the postman who met his death in Northumberland Avenue through impact with a lady in search of her Maker.

Helipads are not open to the public. Safety netting prevents (un)intentional falls from the platform, a feature rarely added to the balcony. Despite the often-visible safety measures, its distance from ground level makes the helipad difficult for passers-by to identify. The crow's nest constructed for the Burj Al Arab and the construction of helipads at lower roof levels restores this visibility, and some designs allow helipads at buildings without a flat roof. Still the highest helipads are located on the flat roofs of skyscrapers, hidden from view and little used.

The helipad welcomes the wealthy, according to its film image. Unfortunately, insurance demands limit landings on Los Angeles helipads. If helicopter landings depend on structural traffic congestion in São Paulo, which is a much reiterated statement about helipads by Paulistas, then helipads should show much more activity in São Paulo than today's flight movements suggest.

The helipad is reduced to a welcoming H, a place of anticipated travel. It is not an ostentatious display of wealth, since the structure goes largely unnoticed unless helicopters make their presence and its presence known. Only helicopters remain associated with importance and wealth, while the grass lawn or the rooftop helipad merely anticipates an event. The rare helicopter travel to the more noticeable helipad designs indicates that the helipad has become an architectural novelty rather than a rich man's accessory.

Welcoming the architect

The purpose of high-rise helipads is to allow helicopter landings in case of emergency or in the rare instance of a visitor. The architect has added the crow's nest construction in Dubai and Seoul to emphasize the shape of the sail, while the Menara Telekom building in Kuala Lumpur resembles a bamboo shoot that provides a lower level roof for a helipad. This use of helipads, that is, to augment the shape and meaning of the building, adds to the multiple uses of helipads that have now led to architectural innovations in helipad construction.

This chapter has not concentrated on helicopter services, but on architects and their patrons who are encouraged and discouraged by city and country regulations to develop helicopter landing sites. If such landing sites extend beyond the conversion of the occasional croquet lawn, then their interest is not found in the optimization of flight movements, but rather in the integration or the contrast of helipad and building design.

In this final chapter, the locations of and reasons for helidromes reappear in a modest attempt to condense the diverse and conflicting data on where and why they were constructed. Helidrome architecture is highlighted with the help of a typology: an explorative summary of and a starting point for the appreciation of helicopter platforms.

— To whom it still concerns

Airports were envisioned on roofs prior to the introduction of helicopters. As soon as helipads were constructed, they were placed on ship decks and roof-tops. The post office roof was first, and was soon followed by the garage and the high-rise building.

Ground-based and elevated helipads are found at hospitals, city heliports, light-houses, office buildings, houses, and hotels. Each group of helipads, with the exception of those on oilrigs and ships, appears with examples of both.

From the perspective of safe helicopter operations, a helipad is placed on top rather than next to a building. Any platform near a building does not have a clear flight path or a view in all directions, and may even suffer from turbulence caused by the building's structure. For reasons of safety, the top of a building is to be preferred in any built-up area.

Once the top of the building is selected, the roofpad often requires a second elevation. The helipad, once more for reasons of safety, has a predetermined size, and requires an unobstructed flight path and view. A narrow roof requires the helipad to extend beyond the roof perimeters, which requires additional support implements. Roof access facilities require the helipad to be raised above the flat surface of the roof. Placing the helipad a number of feet above roof level (ARL) allows the helipad to rise above the other roof amenities, such as air-conditioning units, water basins, and antennas. Hospital roofpads with their need for elevators or ramps cannot always raise their helipads to an optimum height, and often have obstructions still in place. The continuous building activities at hospitals have the helipad move from roof to roof. If investments allow a large ramp or specialized elevator construction, then even hospital helipads feature an unobstructed flight path for a helicopter.

In the absence of a flat roof, helipads are constructed next to antennas, on roofs located below the top or even on cantilever constructions extending from the building. All these constructions are to ensure an unobstructed flight path in as many directions as possible in the absence of an ideal location.

The above contradicts Voigt's statement that helicopter platforms on high-rises are used only sparingly, because they are so dangerous.[Voigt 1996:4] Rather, helipads are preferred on top of buildings to avoid danger, and can be found around the world in large numbers.

Large numbers of hospitals, houses and hotels feature ground-based helipads, and the above safety concerns suggest that they are a safety hazard. In most if not all cases, these helipads are located in the countryside, outside cities, and with obvious and spacious approach routes. City heliports in London and New York have been moved into the river to create a similar effect of a flat open space. Most of these locations indicate where the safest or most convenient landing spaces are, and aviation authorities determine the extent to which these need to be marked and cleared.

Helicopters are particularly suited to landing and taking off from sites other than the helidrome. Only buildings and ships require a helipad construction to make a landing possible. The roof and upper deck are commonly the safer option.

Helipads have been built for the arrival and departure of helicopters. But, in some locations flight movements are regular and frequent, while in others they are largely absent. Helipads are built as a base for helicopter operations, in which case they show regular movements. Or, helipads are built independently of helicopter operations, in which case helicopter movements may be absent. In the latter case, helicopter landings are not required for the helipad to fulfil its purpose.

The first group of helipads was discussed in Chapter 3. Their purpose is transport, and their movements are frequent. The scheduled helicopter operations require a base and a predetermined landing spot for sometimes more than one helicopter. Hospitals, particularly in cities, need a clear landing zone, and often need more helipads than helicopters. This group of helipads was also found in Chapter 4, since oilrigs and lighthouse pads facilitate the regular transport of personnel. Even though their respective number of flight movements contrast, both oilrigs and lighthouses feature regular landings, and they were built with their respective helicopter operations in mind.

The second group of helipads, those with irregular and few landings, is the largest in number. They include all helipads installed for evacuations, such as those found in Chapter 5 for Los Angeles or those in an earlier chapter for cruise ships. Flight movements may indicate disaster for ship or building, and it is hoped these helipads are never used for what they are intended.

Helicopter operations may be of a temporary nature. Icebreakers, cruise and navy ships allow reconnaissance flights from their helidecks, but only when the helicopters are on board. Sporting and racing events use helipads for a limited number of days a year. Office buildings in São Paulo invite the helicopter as a regular taxi, depending on the occupants. The Getty Center once had helicopter operations present when there were forest fires in the vicinity. The use of these helipads changes from evacuation decks to regular heliport to unused space with a windsock. The intention with which helipads are built is not necessarily consistent with their eventual use. Even the first group of helipads may experience a change in purpose. As soon as operations cease, the helipad may still be operational and serve a different purpose.

A helipad may be constructed without helicopter operations as its focus, and may persist when operations are terminated. In other words, helicopter landings and take-offs are optional for a helipad. It is only the possibility of flight movements that makes them helipads.

Helicopters in films play a secondary role, frequently associated with wealth and prestige. Important passengers, exotic locations, and elegant pilots enforce their wealthy image. The helipad seems to play a similar part when it is placed on roofs within the expensive confines of the city, when it is infrequently used for leisure, or frequently used with an ostentatious display of helicopters.

A display of wealth requires an audience. Architects, critics, historians, and

← E-tower, São Paulo, Brazil
(Photo: courtesy of Aflalo &
Gasperini)
↓ Condomínio Edifício
Spazio JK, São Paulo,
Brazil

pedestrians largely ignore the helipad, and in most cases cannot even see the helipad unless a helicopter gives its location away. The expense of a helicopter outweighs the expense of most if not all helipads, particularly when twin-engine helicopters are required for city operations.

The association with wealth is further contradicted by, for instance, the luxury country hotels in Britain that invariably place their helipads on the ground with a minimum or an absence of markings. It is the helicopter and its passengers that may display their wealth on occasion; the helipad is only an inviting letter н.

Instead, helicopters mostly transport personnel to offshore locations, tourists in a circle, and doctors to patients or patients to hospital. None of which are strongly associated with wealth and prestige.

The private villa, luxury yacht, and the skyscraper are prestigious by themselves. In the first two cases, the helicopter is only one of many ostentatious features. In the few known examples, the helipads, if visible at all, are little different from those found on other buildings and ships. Only the helicopter itself, when prominently displayed, adds prestige.

Skyscrapers feature helipads just as rarely as villas and yachts do. Again, it is a secondary feature, and it is difficult to distinguish from an observation deck or a flat roof. The skyscraper is not part of a competition for the tallest helipad; the tallest helipad in the Eastern Hemisphere is not advertised and probably not even known to the building owners and occupants. But, in the last five years, architects have started to give attention to skyscraper helipad designs. The present flight movements suggest that the architects have no particular helicopter operation in mind. They use the helipad to highlight structural features of the building.

It is not impossible that a helipad may be constructed for prestige and a display of wealth. The connection is, in light of the data provided, neither obvious nor automatic. The shifting purpose of helipads indicates that this image of wealth and prestige is generated by the kind of helicopter operations rather than by the helipad construction and design.

— A typology of helidromes

The architecture of helidromes is visibly distinctive. A typology of helipads highlights this distinction. It brings a summarized exploration of helipad architecture; it shows examples of innovations in structure, shape and material in helipad design; it identifies structures that cannot be mistaken for just a flat roof. Such a formal typology is hardly complete or definite, since helipads are continuously being built. The frequency of construction and destruction is much higher than that of airports, and this makes the worldwide distribution of helipads difficult to track.

The architects and designs that are not mentioned in this typology are not inferior. Their results are more difficult to distinguish from other structures, at least from a ground perspective, or are not meant to be visible at all. Square helipads within the perimeter of a roof are not included. Only when the roof design points at the presence of a helipad will the roof design as a whole be considered part of an original type.

→ Renaissance Hotel,
São Paulo, Brazil
↘ Telefónica building,
São Paulo, Brazil
↓ Torre 2000 building,
São Paulo, Brazil

Architectural ideas for helipads are not necessarily related to the support structure. In 1996, Ruy Ohtake delivered the tall Renaissance Hotel in São Paulo, Brazil. Two red towers and a glass middle section support its narrow roof. The two towers hide the roof appliances inside an open space within the grey walls of the top section. The middle section appears as a bridge between the towers with a platform of eighteen by eighteen metres, which fits exactly in this space. The helipad is not raised on a support structure, nor does it tower above the building. The Renaissance Hotel claims to be one of the highest venues in the city, and the helipad covers a reception area. It is part of an idea to have helipads become part of reception areas using their superior view. Ohtake implemented this idea earlier for an office building and a house. The helipad on the Edemar Cid Ferreira Residence, completed in August 2004, is covered in mosaic tiles that double as a reception floor. The protective railing for the guests can be hinged down to transform the artwork into a helicopter landing area. It integrates the reception of parties and helicopters.

Botti Rubin architects in São Paulo were asked to construct a helipad for the Telefónica Company after the final design and construction of the building had been completed. They had to use the existing structure to support the large steel helipad. Their steel was painted red, so that not only the building material, but also the colour of the helipad would contrast the remainder of the building. This idea of contrasting material and colour is found repeatedly. Carlos Bratke designed and built a red-and-yellow helipad for the Attílio Tinelli building; it was conceived after the design and construction of the underlying building had already been completed. One of the latest designs by Ruy Ohtake, the Ohtake Cultural in São Paulo created in 2003, also has a red helipad in place; this time the idea was implemented before the start of any building activities. So far, the colour red appears to be the preferred contrast in these examples.

Contrasts in shape are more common. They mostly include the entire roof. Ruy Ohtake completed the Joaquim Floriano 100 building in 2002. The blue glass façade attracts attention for its bright red column that houses the elevator. The red column appears a free-standing column at the entrance where the front blue glass is cut away, and pedestrians can pass underneath. The blue glass has been removed symmetrically on the upper part of the building leaving two balconies at either side of the red column. Over the full length of the building a hovering roof appears, clearly not touching the red column, and supported in such a way that it appears from all sides to be a hovering roof. It creates all the space needed for the roof amenities, including a platform. A windsock on the corner of the roof gives its presence away but only the back half of the roof is needed for the platform. The helipad is small, measuring only 12×12 metres, but still allows 4 tons. It only had two winching activities in the last one-and-a-half years. Since hovering roofs are common, only the windsock points at a helipad.

When Jonas Birger started the Torre 2000 Building, a square 24×24-metre platform was conceived to allow the largest helicopters to land. The building was to have a round roof, in sharp contrast to the rest of the building. Yet, a circle around a 24×24-metre platform has a diameter of at least 34 metres, and this appeared too exaggerated for the size of the building. Jonas Birger and his consulting engineer Carlos Freire opted for the 21×21 metre platform still allowing the second largest helicopter in operation, an Aerospatiale Dauphin, to make a landing. Nevertheless, the size of the Torre 2000 roof was to attract attention from the entire neighbourhood. The circle structure, which was partly constructed with aluminium, was to be 'o coroamento do edifício' or the crown of the building.Finestra 2002 Only in São Paulo can such a metal roof immediately be associated with the presence of a helipad, to the outsider it is not a matter of course.

All these examples of helipad appearance do not mark the construction as unique to helidrome architecture. They are highlights rather than separately conceived constructions. They are roofs accommodating helipads and not featuring helipads. The following constructions point at unique helipad shapes and forms. They are the basis for a helidrome typology.

The steel wafer

The wafer is part of most rooftop helipads. The steel construction invariably appears as a wafer, but, depending on its support structure, it is not always visible as such. Apart from being thin and flat, the wafer also displays a net-like structure. This is best exemplified by the lighthouse lantern pads that feature safety netting on the outer perimeter, and often show an open steel platform through which the wind may pass unobstructed.

The steel wafer is easily confused with other overhanging roofs. Only the material suggests a difference, such as rope netting or a hovering thin steel slab. The support structure commonly adds to the effect, but, since overhanging roofs may feature similar structures underneath, this cannot be its only differentiating feature.

The ideal steel wafer type is visible from all sides. The support structure highlights its presence, and its mace-like structure avoids any confusion with other roof constructions. The helipad on a typical high-rise building rarely attains these characteristics, unless a pronounced pedestal is installed upon the roof.

In 1982, a five-star hotel was commissioned on an area of more than 2,000 square metres on the river Rio in Belo Horizonte, Brazil. It became known as the Beira-Rio or the Palace Hotel. The full space is used for the partly underground parking garage. The hotel floors, up to around seventy-five metres, use an area of 1,170 square metres for rooms, suites, bars, and restaurants. Suites and swimming pools occupy the upper floors with two heated pools and a semi-Olympic swimming pool on the top floor.

At 81.5 metres above ground, a one-and-a-half-metre wide ramp gives access to a separate structure on the top of the roof. The ramp is designed to circumvent a water tank with a capacity of 250 cubic metres. At 87.80 metres the ramp ends, and reaches a 256-square-metre helipad.

The architect, Miguel Morante Garcia from Spain, specified the above in a descriptive memo for his client. It does not specify that the helipad allows 20 tons of weight for the helicopters, and that the ramp around the water tank is wide enough for a car and is surrounded by a transparent wall. The ramp is supposed to be lit, and it should turn the top of the building into a lantern towering above the city of Belo Horizonte.

The building was partly finished with a large helipad already constructed when

Millennium Park helipad:
aerial view (Photo: courtesy
of Botti Rubin Arquitetos)
← Atrium, Tenenge building,
São Paulo, Brazil (Photo:
courtesy of Botti Rubin
Arquitetos)
↗ Millennium Park helipad:
park view (Photo: courtesy of
Botti Rubin Arquitetos)
→ Helipad construction of
the Millennium Park building
as designed by the archi-
tects (Drawing: courtesy of
Botti Rubin Arquitetos)
→→ Millennium Park heli-
pad: street view

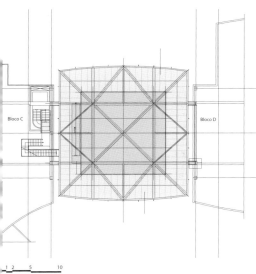

Bloco C

Bloco D

1 2   5   10

funding ceased. The neighbourhood did not make this five-star hotel a promising prospect for other investors. The deserted building is now closed to the public. A laundry service briefly occupied the lower floors, later followed by squatters and circumspect businesses. A large police force removed the unwanted occupants a few years ago, and today only police helicopters use the facilities — they practice rooftop approaches.

Even though the ramp is not lit, and the building is not finished, the Beira-Rio Hotel with its towering helipad can be seen from large parts of the city. The load factor of 20 tons is the highest for any roof pad in Brazil.

The road leading up to the top indicates that people are moved to and from the roof. The staircase on the side of the helipad of Hotel Mélia has a similar effect. Even the staircase of the Ft. Lauderdale heliport indicates a special entrance different from the car park entrances on the lower levels. Such elements set the wafer type apart from constructions for elevator shafts or access rooms to the main roof.

The atrium

The atrium is a roof between two buildings. It sits between the amenities of rooftops without interference. Botti Rubin in São Paulo first conceived this solution for their Tenenge building, constructed between 1974–1978.[Botti, Rubin & Otmar 2003] It is a tall building and the helipad is hardly part of the pedestrian experience of the building's architecture.

This changed with the Millennium Park project, which started in 2000 and was completed in 2004 by Botti Rubin Arquitetos.[Finestra 2004] The low-rise buildings of this office complex feature an atrium. The helipad has become the roof of the entry road, delivering a grand entrance. This atrium construction appears not so much a solution that bypasses roof amenities, but also allows a helicopter approach route that is not easily obstructed by future high-rise buildings in the vicinity of the complex. The helipad is centred between offices, optimizing the space between the helipad and later buildings.

The atrium solution highlights the position and the function of the helipad. Its presence dominates the building design. Botti Rubin had included an elegant and resilient steel support structure of the helipad visible to pedestrians. Unfortunately, the building contractors opted for a cheaper solution. The result is still unique in helipad design history and majestic in its appearance.

The cantilever

The cantilever roof is not unique to helipads, and neither is the hovering roof, although its name may suggest otherwise. The hovering roof commonly uses a cantilever construction or a 'French hand', as it is known in Brazil. Frank Lloyd Wright, who never had a helipad in mind, frequently constructed such roofs. The effect of Wright's roofs is markedly different from cantilever constructions recently designed for helipads.

Ruy Ohtake constructed a hovering roof on the Floriano building, where the cantilever construction does not outsize the building. Instead, a gap in the building is created. The roof overhangs the building, and the building overhangs the entrance. The roof has a helipad, but the support construction is not immediately or necessarily associated with the presence of a helipad.

Joaquim Floriano 100 building,
São Paulo, Brazil
← Cantilever, London City
Heliport (Computer animation:
Foster & Sons)

↖ Half-pipe, Attílio Tinelli building
← Construction of the Attílio
Tinelli helipad, São Paulo, Brazil
(Photo: courtesy of Carlos
Dumont)
↑ Banespa building, Praça da
Republica, São Paulo, Brazil
(Photo: courtesy of Carlos Bratke)
↗ Escritórios Berrini Lavra with
an inverted dome on the roof,
São Paulo, Brazil
→ Nidec Head Quarters and
Central Technical Laboratory,
Kyoto, Japan

Sir Norman Foster suggested another type of cantilever construction for his London heliport. This construct showed transparency and lightness, since only the area on the rooftop needed to be large. The offices underneath occupy a smaller floor area. The entire construct is a heliport, and there is no confusion as to the roof's purpose. It contrasts with most other riverside heliport designs that are placed in or on the water or hover just above the waterline. Foster adds height, and its overhanging structure above water is as yet unrepeated.

The steel overhanging cantilever roof is often so dominant on a building structure that it can rarely be mistaken for something else. Even a concrete overhanging construction points to a helipad, such as the E-tower helipad designed by Aflalo & Gasperini in São Paulo or the helipad on the California Bank Trust in Los Angeles. Hovering roofs, such as Edo Rocha's Condomínio Edifício Spazio JK, are often integrated in the building design, and do not necessarily point to the helipad's existence. It is therefore not the hovering, but the overhanging cantilever roof that appears to stand out as a construction specific to rooftop helipads.

The half-pipe

The half-pipe is a curved construction. Although it is possible to introduce this structure into a roof garden or observation deck, it has been exclusively designed for helipads. The half-pipe slightly raises the helipad above the roof so that reinforcement of the roof underneath is possible, while roof amenities occupy other parts of the roof. The half-pipe does not appear as a shaft extending from the building below, since the visible contact area with the roof is minimized. In conjunction these features make the half-pipe an ideal shape for helipads, and markedly different from other possible amenities and facilities on a roof.

Carlos Bratke developed half-pipe roof constructions. He is a São Paulo architect known for his many office buildings in Brazil, and one of the prolific Brazilian architects of today. Despite his long record, he has constructed only few helipads. At least three constructions with the appearance of a half-pipe have been developed, but not all for helipads. The first was the 1992 Banespa building at Praça da República in São Paulo. It received much attention for its terrace-shaped floors. The half-pipe is not rounded, but terraced like the rest of the building. The half-pipe is not continued at the back, making it a half half-pipe, and appears to be only a prelude. The Escritórios Berrini Lavra building is also located in São Paulo, and was completed in 1995.[ProjetoDesign 1997:42–45] It does not feature a helipad and the original design was dome-shaped, the opposite of a half-pipe. The dome appeared too costly and was inverted. The helipad on the Attílio Tinelli building in São Paulo was completed in 2002, and uses red and yellow to emphasize the contrast with the rest of the building.[Finestra 2000, Boschetti 2003] This helipad is a complete half-pipe, and seems to stand alone on the building top. The earlier designs by Bratke were boxed in by other roof structures. No helipad on the building was envisioned on the original drawings and computer animations; the helipad was designed after the design and construction of the building had already been finished.[Wissenbach 1999:138, 222, 223] The half-pipe is a helipad type first developed by a Brazilian architect and

nowadays also found in Japan. The Nidec building on the outside of the city of Kyoto has a helipad on its 100 metres tall roof. Completed in March, 2004, by Mr Hojo of the Toshi Kyoju Bunka Kenkyojo in Kyoto, it is proudly visible next to the Shinkansen train tracks but has no helicopter movements to date.

The half-pipe is not a structure for the convenience of pilots — the square alternative is cheaper and the Attílio Tinelli building hardly has any flight movements to boast. Its prestige is raised by the architect, not because of its relation to helicopters, but because the helipad draws attention to the design of the building. The architecture, rather than the helicopter, creates prestige.

The mound

The mound is nothing short of a mountain. It could be a mountain with the top cut off as exemplified by Onassis's mountain on Skorpios. Hill tops and raised parts in the landscape are often preferred helicopter landings spots. For instance, the helispot Mirante Dona Marta near Rio de Janeiro's Corcovado is a hill top that doubles as a tourist observation post. The mound type is simply an exaggerated man-made hill with a flattened top.

The only designer mound for helicopters is probably the helipad at the Getty Center constructed by Richard Meier. This earthen mound has an ideally-sized flat round top and a strong base to support a helicopter. The Getty Center does not require a helipad. The centre, located on top of a hill on the outskirts of Los Angeles, consists of a series of smaller buildings. At each extremity a round towering structure is found. On one side it houses a cactus garden, and on the other it is a helipad. The helipad is a simple round area of grass with a two feet depression or moat surrounding it. The hill itself is solid and covered with a layer of stones, the same type used on most of the other buildings.

Helicopter landings are few and far between. It is known that helicopters landed at the Getty Center during great forest fires.Lisa Klikoff 2004, pers. comm. The Getty has large water supplies that were used to supply the helicopters. Despite the opulence of the Getty, the helicopters do not regularly bring dignitaries, nor are they required for medical assistance purposes. The Getty does not house a helicopter on its premises either. The helipad is simply Richard Meier's idea of contrasting a cactus garden with a round lawn, the purpose of which is identified by one sign, a windsock; there is no H. But as long as the cacti are not growing at the centre, it is difficult to imagine another purpose for a perfect grass circle on top of a hill.

So far the mound type is one of few original designs for ground-based helipads.

The crow's nest

The crow's nest is supported by a limited number of beams or pipes, commonly three, extending from the building to the helipad. The buildings by Tom Watts and Sir Norman Foster in Dubai and Seoul, respectively, extend the helipad sideways from the building. This construction, similar to cantilever constructions, is also found on oilrigs, and makes the helipad more readily accessible for the pilot and more easily visible from the ground. The exposed nature of a sideways-extended helipad, the thin plateau and the absence of fences set it apart from observation decks.

Crow's nest, Herbis Plaza
Ent', Osaka, Japan
Next page: Mound, Getty
Center

Table of types

* It is yet unknown which place in the world was first decorated with a capital H, but different countries use different symbols. For instance, the P for private, the M for military and the H for hospital pads are used in Brazil.

** Foster conceived helipad designs of different types. It has made him one of few Western European architects extensively involved in helipad design, perhaps because he flies helicopters himself (Caroline Pack 2004, personal communication).

Type	Building	Location	Architect	Year	Symbol
Helipad*	—	—	—	—	H
Steel wafer	Lighthouse	Wolf Rock	Trinity House	1973	T
Atrium	High-rise	São Paulo	Botti Rubin	1974	π
Cantilever	Heliport	London	Norman Foster**	1988	Γ
Half-pipe	Office	São Paulo	Carlos Bratke	1992	⊃
Mound	Museum	Los Angeles	Richard Meier	1997	∩
Crow's nest	Skyscraper	Dubai	Tom Watts	1999	Y

A crow's nest that rises upwards from a building has also been referred to as a torch. The Olympic torch is often presented on a three-legged pedestal, and resembles a miniature helipad of this kind. In 1979, Sir Norman Foster presented a design for an unbuilt structure known as the Hammersmith Centre, London.^{Chaslin & Hervet & Lavalou 1990:68} Ken Yeang did the same for the Armory Tower, which was first conceived in 1997, and is planned in Shanghai.^{Powell 1999:92–97} The Takenaka Corporation in Japan constructed a group of buildings in central Osaka. Completed in November, 2005, the Herbis Plaza Ent' houses restaurants and entertainment facilities. It received a torch-shape helipad on the roof. Just as the other helipads recently constructed on Japanese high-rise buildings, the platform features no helicopter movements,

The crow's nest, contrary to a cantilever construction as described earlier, is separated from the building. It is an attachment that places the helipad in space away from the building. The steel wafer has a solid base; the crow's nest is supported by arms that extend upwards or sideways.

It is possible to invent constructions that blur the divisions between crow's nest, cantilever and wafer, but at present they have clear individual characteristics.

Table of types

The above table lists the types of helipads, and suggests some typographical signs for identification. One example illustrates each type, and in some cases is the first example of its kind in city architecture.

The beginning

Architectural historians have not yet found much to say about the helipad. Architects mention its height, sometimes its size, but in large measure do not have much else to share. Raving reviews of rare heliport architecture are perhaps rightfully absent.

But meanwhile architects have solved problems that helipads created, and made choices concerning their designs. The helipad is visible or invisible from the ground, integrates or contrasts with the roof, shares or displaces other roof amenities, is recognizable as a helipad or is incognito. In some cities, the helipad appears instead of observation decks or a plain flat roof. The helipad then becomes a roof option rather than a helicopter facility, and this helipad can be original, complex, and even beautiful.

The ostentatious helipad is largely absent, which is not consistent with the imagery of helicopters. A helipad, contrary to a helicopter, rarely stands out as a symbol of power, wealth, and exotic location. The limited use that is made of, for instance, Bratke's half-pipe and Tom Watts's crow's nest illustrates that the transport function of these helipads is secondary. If the helipad is not necessarily used for transport and hardly used as a symbol of wealth and prestige, what explains its existence?

The answer is found in a possibility rather than a reality. The helidrome gives helicopters access to a location. Accessibility is its primary purpose. In most cases access is restricted to specific helicopter operations. General access is rarely attained, with the occasional exception of helidromes with a public transport function. Most helidromes allow helicopter visits in times of emergency, which is one of few helicopter operations to which restrictions rarely apply. The Brazilian distinction between private, military and hospital helidromes indicates that access to, in this case Brazilian, helipads is restricted as soon as the helipad is in operation. The usefulness of the helidrome is found in access to a location, but the use of the helidrome is restricted to a specific kind of helicopter operation that may change over time.

Like Panamarenko's objects, the helipad is by definition useful, but not necessarily put to use. If not in use, the helipad remains accessible. A helipad highlights the symbolism or the symmetry or the originality of the building; it allows emergency airlifts or special transports from an otherwise flat surface; it can even act as a stabilizer during earthquakes. Once this multi-purpose task of helipads is understood, the idea of the helidrome is not as flat and unchanging as the aviation definitions suggest. The architects have only just begun.

References

Abreu, Alex 2005. Cartão-Postal. *Casa, V.237, pp.128–135.*

American Aviation 1943a. Skyway Crop. Applies for helicopter lines. *American Aviation, June 15, 1943, p.46.*

American Aviation 1943b. Sikorsky to set up helicopter airport. *American Aviation, July 1, 1943, p.72.*

American Aviation 1947. First helicopter route OK'd by CAB. *American Aviation, June 15, 1947, p.13.*

American Aviation 1948. Bright future for 'Copter found in L.A. experiment. *American Aviation, June 1, 1948, p.20.*

Anderson, John D. 1997. *A history of aerodynamics.* Cambridge University Press: Cambridge.

André, Valérie 1988. *Madame le Général.* Paris: Perrin.

Arroyo, José 2000. *Action/spectacle Cinema: a sight and sound reader.* London: BFI Publishing.

Baker III, A.D. 2000. *The Naval Institute guide to combat fleets of the world 2000–2001: their ships, aircraft, and systems.* Annapolis, MD: Naval Institute Press.

Bartlett, Arthur 1944. Remember Lidice. *Los Angeles Times, October 22, 1994, p.F6.*

Baumunk, Bodo-Michael 1996. *Die Kunst des Fliegens: Malerei, Skulptur, Architektur, Fotografie, Literatur, Film.* Friedrichshafen: Zeppelin-Museum.

Bellour, Raymond 2000. *The analysis of film.* [Edited by Constance Penly] Bloomington: Indiana University Press.

BHAB (British Helicopter Advisory Board) 2004. *Information handbook 2004/2005.* Chobham, Woking.

Binder, George (ed.) 2001. *Tall buildings of Asia & Australia.* Melbourne: The Images Publishing Group Pty Ltd.

Bloomfield, Howard V.L. 1966. *The compact history of the United States coast guard.* New York: Hawthorn Books.

Boesiger, Willy 1961. *Le Corbusier: oeuvre complète 1938–1946.* Fourth edition. Zurich: Editions Girsberger.

Boesiger, Willy 1965. *Le Corbusier et son atelier rue de Sèvres 35: oeuvre complète 1957–1965.* Zurich: Les Editions d'Architecture (Artemis).

Boschetti, Joe (ed.) 2003. *Details in architecture: creative detailing by some of the world's leading architects.* Melbourne, Australia: Images Publishing Group.

Botti, Alberto & Marc Rubin & Renee Otmar (eds.) 2003. *Botti Rubin Arquitetos: selected and current works.* Melbourne, Australia: Images Publishing Group.

Branch, Melville C. 1973. *Urban air traffic and city planning: case study of Los Angeles County.* London: Pall Mall Press.

Bray, Dorothy (ed.); in collaboration with the White Mountain Apache Tribe 1998. *Western Apache–English Dictionary: a community-generated bilingual dictionary.* Tempe, Arizona: Bilingual Press.

Bristow, Alan E. 1956. Helicopter operations in the Persian Gulf. *The Journal of the Helicopter Association of Great Britain, V.10, No.1, pp.3–23.*

Brooks, Tim & Earle Marsh 1988. *The complete directory to prime-time network tv shows: 1946–present.* Fourth edition. New York: Ballantine Books.

Brown, Captain Eric M. 1981. *The helicopter in civil operations.* New York: Van Nostrand Reinhold Company.

Butler, Daniel Allen 2003. *The age of Cunard: a transatlantic history 1839–2004.* Lighthouse Press: Annapolis, Maryland.

Byron, Robert 1928. *The station. Athos: treasures and men.* London: Duckworth Press.

Cafarakis, Christian 1971. *Onassis: zijn leven en liefdes.* [Translated from Le Fabuleux Onassis] Baarn: Meulenhoff.

CBS 2002. *Kengetallen.* Centraal Bureau voor de Statistiek: Den Haag.

Celebrity Cruises Press Office 2002 (May 13). *Celebrity Cruises Launches New Constellation Fourth in Series of Four Millennium-class Vessels Sets Sail from Barcelona.*

Central Airports Ltd. 1933. *The London Airport and Marketing Centre.* Pamphlet.

Chapman, James 1999. *License to thrill: a cultural history of the James Bond films.* London: J.B. Taurus Publishers.

Chaslin, Francois & Frédérique Hervet & Armelle Lavalou 1990 (1986). *Norman Foster.* Paris: Electa Moniteur.

Cie. Hef. (Commissie Hefschroefvliegtuigen). 1954. *Literatuuroverzicht inzake luchtvaartterreinen voor hefschroefvliegtuigen.* Algemeen Rijksarchief Den Haag, Tweede Afdeling, Archief van de Commissie Hefschroefvliegtuigen, 1953–1956, Inventory No. 2.16.34 (18).

CNN (Environmental News Network) 1998. *Japan begins 12th 'scientific' whale hunt.* www.cnn.com/TECH/science/9811/10/japan.whaling.yoto/. Extracted 31 may 2004.

Cohen, Jean-Louise 1995. Van hangars naar luchthavens. In: Diane Hennebert etc., *Luchttuigen 1900–1958 & Panamarenko, pp.64–73.* Wetteren, Belgium: Cultura.

Cowdrey, C.F. & D.W. Bryer 1973 (March). *Measurements of the time-average forces and pitching moments on a proposed helicopter landing platform for the Wolf Rock Lighthouse.* Department of Trade and Industry: Division of Maritime Science.

Dawson, Ned 2005. Burj-eoning business. *HeliOps International, V.35, pp.*14–25.

Delear, Frank J. 1969. *Igor Sikorsky: his three careers in aviation.* New York: Dodd, Mead & Company.

Dellaert, U.F.M. 1954. *Onderzoek inzake de meest geschikte plaats voor een helihaven in Amsterdam.* Amsterdam: Gemeentearchief.

Dumas, Olivier 2000. *Voyage à travers Jules Verne: biographie.* Montréal: Alain Stanké.

Emporis 2004. Emporis Data Commission. Statistics extracted on June 27, 2004 from *www.emporis.com.* Definitions extracted August 31, 2004 from *www.emporis.com/en/ab/ds/sg/ra/bu/de/hi/.*

Farmer, James 1949. *Celluloid Wings: the impact of movies on aviation.* Blue Ridge Summit, PA.

Férey, Sylvia 1995. Luchthaven van Bamako. In: Diane Hennebert etc.,

Luchttuigen 1900–1958 & *Panamarenko, pp.*76–77. Wetteren, Belgium: Cultura.

Ferrari, Pierre & Jacques M. Vernet 1984. *Une guerre sans fin: Indochine 1945–1954.* Paris: Lavauzelle.

Finestra 2000. Desenho prismático. *Finestra Brasil, V.*6, *October, pp.*72–76. São Paulo.

Finestra 2002. Cristal, pedra e aeronaves no topo. *Finestra Brasil, V.*32, *January.* São Paulo.

Finestra 2004. Heliponto ganha destaque. *Finestra Brasil, V.*37, *April, pp.*55–61. São Paulo.

Flight 1950. [Untitled] *Flight, V.*57, *No.* 2161, *pp.*622,631,548. [also known as *Flight and Aircraft Engineer*, founded in 1909, published in London.]

Flight 1951. Stop to think. *Flight, V.*60, *No.*2231, *p.*547.

Flight 1952. Airstop, helidrome or rotorstation? *Flight, V.*62, *No.*2286, *p.*611.

Franquinet, E. 1942. *Jules Verne: zijn persoon en zijn werk.* Eindhoven: NV Uitgeversmaatschappij De Pelgrim.

Froesch, Charles & Walther Prokosch 1946. *Airport planning.* New York: John Wiley & Sons, Inc.

Froman, Frances & Alfred Keye & Lottie Keye & Carrie J. Dyck 2002. *English–Cayuga, Cayuga–English dictionary.* Toronto: University of Toronto Press.

Frost, John B. 1996. *British helipads.* Chester: Appledore Publications.

Fulbright, J. William 1970. *The Pentagon propaganda machine.* New York: Liveright.

Garland, Brock 1987. *War movies.* New York: Facts on File Publications.

Garnham, Nicholas 1971. *Samuel Fuller.* London: Secker & Warburg Ltd.

Geiger, Hermann 1955. *Pilote des glaciers.* Arthaud: Paris.

Geldhof, N. 1987. *70 Jaar Marineluchtvaartdienst.* Leeuwarden: Uitgeverij Eisma BV.

Giedion, Sigfried 1956. Brazil and contemporary architecture. In: Henrique E. Mindlin, *Modern architecture in Brazil, pp.ix–x.* Rio de Janeiro/ Amsterdam: Colibris Editora Ltda.

Giedion, Sigfried 1967. *Space, time and architecture: the growth of a new tradition.* Cambridge, Massachusetts: Harvard University Press.

Gilman, Rhoda R. (ed.) 1969. *A Yankee Inventor's flying ship — two pamphlets by Rufus Porter.* St. Paul: Minnesota Historical Society.

Goldstein, Laurence 1986. *The flying machine and modern literature.* London: Macmillan Press.

Guilbert, Louis 1965. *Glossaire de l'aviation de 1861 à 1891. Tome second de la thèse: la formation du vocabulaire de l'aviation.* Paris.

Gunnarsson, S. 1999. Malmo/Copenhagen. In: RAES Proceedings 19 October 1999, *The potential of rotorcraft to increase airport capacity, pp.*1.1–1.6. London: Royal Aeronautical Society.

HAGB 1958. *Examination of the case for a London Heliport.* London. Pamphlet of 16 pages.

Haneveld, G.T. 1959. Enkele medische ervaringen in Libanon met de kleine helicopter Bell H13. *Nederlands Militair Geneeskundig Tijdschrift V.*3, *p.*66–69.

Harlaftis, Gelina 1996. *A history of Greek-owned shipping: the making of an international tramp fleet, 1830 to the present day.* London: Routledge.

Healey, Andrew 2003. *Leading from the front: Bristow Helicopters, the first 50 years.* Stroud, Gloucestershire: Tempus.

Hill, J.R. 1972. *The United States Coast Guard.* London: The Atlantic Education Trust.

Holmes, Donald B. 1981. *Air mail: an illustrated history 1793–1981.* New York: Clarkson N. Potter, Inc./Publishers.

Horonjeff, Robert & Francis X. McKelvey 1994 (fourth edition). *Planning and design of airports.* New York: McGraw Hill.

Horsley, Carter B. 2003 (updated from 1998). *The Metlife building (the former Pan Am Building).* Extracted from www.thecityreview.com/panam.html on June 9, 2004.

HSAC 2004. *Gulf of Mexico offshore helicopter operational data summary.* Extracted 29 May 2004 from www.hsac.org/2003stats.htm.

ICAO 1995. *Heliport manual.* Montreal, Canada: ICAO Publications.

Jonge, Lex de & Marc Konijn 2006. Niet in maar bóven de file: voor tachtig euro met de helikopter van Utrecht naar Amsterdam. *Algemeen Dagblad, August 1, pp.6–7.*

Kagan, Norman 1974. *The war film.* New York: Pyramid.

Kalter, Suzy 1984. *The complete book of M*A*S*H.* New York: Abradale Press.

Kasindorf, Martin 1976. James Gavin: directing in the air. *Action V.11, No.3, pp.16–23.*

Kelly, Fred C. 1940 (1943). *The Wright Brothers: a biography authorized by Orville Wright.* New York: Ballantine Books.

Lam, David M. 1988. To pop a balloon: aeromedical evacuations in the 1870 siege of Paris. *Aviation, Space and Environmental Medicine V.59, pp.988–991.*

Law, Harvey F. 1957. Helicopter operations of the Port of the New York Authority. *Journal of the American Helicopter Society V.2, No.3, pp.15–18.*

Le Corbusier 1935. *Aircraft.* London: The Studio.

Leeuwen, Thomas A.P. van 1986. *The skyward trend of thought.* The Hague: AHA books.

Leishman, J. Gordon 2000. *Principles of helicopter aerodynamics.* Cambridge University Press: Cambridge.

Lipman, Jean 1968. *Rufus Porter — Yankee pioneer.* New York: Clarkson N. Potter.

Lipstadt, Hélène 2004. Co-making the modern monument: The Jefferson National Expansion Memorial Competition and Eero Saarinen's Gateway Arch. In: Eric Mumford (ed.) *Modern architecture in St. Louis: Washington University and postwar American architecture 1948–1973, pp.4–24.* Washington University in St. Louis: School of Architecture

Lucas, P. 1966. *Luchthaven en de heliport: 1945 t/m 1965.* Rotterdam: Gemeentearchief Rotterdam.

MacDonald, Edwin A. 1969. *Polar operations.* U.S. Naval Institute: Annapolis, MD.

Marques, Joao Carlos 2003, 2002, 2001, 2000, 1999. *Pilot's Help.* São Paulo.

McClain, Stan 1996. A history of Hollywood's aerial cinematography. *The*

Operating Cameraman, 1996 *Spring Issue*. Toluca Lake, California: Society of Camera Operators.

Metro 2003. Red het oerbos, steun Greenpeace! *Metro, December* 3, 2003, *p.*18.

Metz, Christian 2000. The imaginary signifier. In: Toby Miller and Robert Stam (eds.) *Film and theory: an anthology*. United Kingdom: Blackwell Publishers.

MFB 1953. Glory Brigade, the, U.S.A., 1953. *Monthly Film Bulletin, July* 1953, *V.*20, *No.* 234.

Miles, Marvin 1947. Helicopters speed mail delivery in Southland. *Los Angeles Times, November* 17, 1947, *p.*A1.

Miller, William H. jr. 1981. *The great luxury liners* 1927–1954 — *a photographic record*. New York: Dover Publishing.

Morgan, Bob 1985. Birds over Hollywood. *American Cinematographer V.*66, *No.*8, *pp.*73–76. Hollywood, California.

Neto, Otávio Teixeira de Abreu 2006. *Diretrizes para elaboração de projetos para construção e regularização de heliportos e helipontos*. São Paulo, CEFETSP: Graduate thesis.

New York Times, 1943a. Army says test proves use for helicopters. *May* 26, 1943, *p.*21. New York.

New York Times, 1943b. Helicopters used in U-boat patrols: Capt. L.P. Lovett, Navy public relations chief, sees them as 'secret success'. *April* 21, 1943, *p.*29. New York.

New York Times, 1944. Helicopter rushes plasma to injured: makes jump from Battery to Sandy Hook in 14 minutes, hour trip for boat. *January* 4, 1944, *p.*3. New York.

New York Times, 1948a. Police authorized to buy helicopter for $25,000. *August* 11, 1948, *p.*23. New York.

New York Times, 1948b. Police helicopter helps save 5 trapped by tide on Coney jetty. *October* 24, 1948, *p.*42. New York.

New York Times, 1948c. Police helicopter is tested in rain: addition to Aviation Bureau praised by mayor — designed for sea, land rescue. *October* 1, 1948, *p.*52. New York.

New York Times, 1949. 'Heliport' opened on East River Pier: city's first rotary wing plane base starts operations near Gouverneur Street. *May* 19, 1949, *p.*58. New York.

New York Times, 1951. C.A.B. approves a helicopter line for city area and as airport link: helicopter permit won for city area. *December* 6, 1951, *pp.*1–2. New York.

New York Times, 1951a. Helicopter lands on city building: makes 3 round trips to 8th Ave. from Idlewild as part of engineers meeting. *April* 20, 1951, *p.*38. New York.

New York Times, 1951b. Port Authority helicopter begins routine service: helicopter starts roof service for officials of Port Authority. *June* 1, 1951, *p.*25. New York.

New York Times, 1953. New city heliport opened at Battery: 7 craft fly and hover above Pier A as second municipal facility is dedicated. *June* 12, 1953, *p.*29. New York.

Nicholson, Christopher 2002 (first published 1995). *Rock lighthouses of Britain: the end of an era?* Latheronwheel, Scotland: Whittles Publishing.

NYT, see *New York Times*

O'Ballance, Edgar 1966. *Malaya: the communist insurgent war, 1948–1960.* London: Faber and Faber Ltd.

Paris, Michael 1995. *From the Wright Brothers to Top Gun: aviation, nationalism and popular cinema.* Manchester: Manchester University Press.

Pfeiffer, Bruce Brooks 1990. *Frank Lloyd Wright drawings.* New York: Harry N. Abrams, Inc.

Powell, Robert 1999. *Rethinking the skyscraper: the complete architecture of Ken Yeang.* New York: Whitney Library of Design.

ProjetoDesign 1997. Edifício de escritórios Berrini Lavra. *ProjetoDesign, January*, pp.42–45.

Rees, Elfan A. 2003. Bristow Helicopters: an early history. *Helicopter International V.27, No.2, p.52.*

Ricciardi, Alessia 2000. The spleen of Rome: mourning modernism in Fellini's *La dolce vita. Modernism/Modernity, V.7, No. 2, pp.201–219.*

Ridgeway and Clark Report 1954. *Pictorial history of the Korean war 1950–1953.* Memorial Edition. Veterans' Historical Book Service, Inc: USA.

Robbins, Guy 2001. *The aircraft carrier story 1908–1945.* London: Cassell&Co.

Roberts, Randy & James S. Olson 1995. *John Wayne: American.* New York: The Free Press.

Royal Caribbean Cruiselines Press Office. 2001 (March 21). *Radiance of the Seas arrives in Miami.*

Ruhrfestspiele Recklinghausen 1977. *Fliegen—ein Traum, Faszination, Fortschritt, Vernichtungswahn,* 31. Ruhrfestspiele Recklinghausen: Städtische Kunsthalle Recklinghausen.

Scheers, M.C. 1953. *Het hefschroefvliegtuig: nieuwe verkeers-en vervoersmogelijkheden.* Rapporten en Mededelingen No. 8, September 1953. Rotterdam: Nederlandsch Overzee Instituut.

Schofield, B.B. 1969. Chapter 27. In: Peter Kemp (ed.), *History of the Royal Navy, pp.291–299.* London: Arthur Barker Limited.

Shain, Russell Earl 1976. *An analysis of motion pictures about war released by the American film industry 1930–1970.* Ph.D-thesis. New York: Arno Press.

Skogsberg, Bertil 1981. *Wings on the screen: a pictorial history of air movies.* New York: A.S.Barnes & Co.

Skone J.F. & J. Mills 1960. The seriously ill patient and the helicopter. *The Lancet, V.11, pp.363–364.*

Slikke, W. van der 1964. De helicopter bij het gewonden-en ziekenvervoer. *Het Reddingwezen V.53, No.2, pp.53–55.* Lochem: NV Uitgeversmaatschappij De Tijdstroom.

Stubelius, Svante 1960. *Balloon, Flying-Machine, Helicopter: further studies in the history of terms for aircraft in English.* Acta Universitatis Gothoburgensis, Göteborgs Universitets Årsskrift V.66. Göteborg.

Taves, Brian & Stephen Michaluk, Jr. 1996. *The Jules Verne encyclopedia.* Lanham, Maryland: Scarecrow Press.

Theys, Hans 1992. *Panamarenko*. Tervuren: Exhibitions International.

Unwin, Timothy 2000. The fiction of science, or the science of fiction. In Edmund J. Smyth (ed.), *Jules Verne: narratives of modernity, pp.46–59.* Liverpool: Liverpool University Press.

Van Vleet, Clarke & Lee M. Pearson & Adrian O. Van Wyen 1970 (second edition). *United States Naval Aviation 1910–1970.* Washington: US Government Printing Office.

Ven, Cornelis van de 1978. *Space in architecture: the evolution of a new idea in the theory and history of the modern movements.* Amsterdam: Van Gorcum Assen.

Voigt, Wolfgang 1996. From the hippodrome to the aerodrome, from the air station to the terminal: European airports, 1909–1945. In: John Zukowksy (ed.) *Building for air travel: architecture and design for commercial aviation. pp.27–50.* Chicago: Prestel/The Art Institute of Chicago.

Volkskrant 1984. Plannen voor helihaven bij het IJ in Amsterdam. *August 8, 1984.* Amsterdam.

Volkskrant 2002. Lachend boven de file. *September 9, 2002, p.9.* Amsterdam.

Voogt, Alex de 2006. Hospital helipad architecture: ideals of safety and design. In Cor Wagenaar (ed.) *Hospital Architecture, pp.141–157.* AZG: Groningen.

Ward, Douglas 2004. *Ocean cruising and cruise ships 2004.* London: Berlitz Publishing.

Wissenbach, Vicente (ed.) 1999. *Carlos Bratke: arquiteto/architect.* São Paulo: ProEditores.

Wohl, Robert 1994. *A Passion for Wings: Aviation and the Western Imagination 1908–1918.* New Haven: Yale University Press.

Woodman, Richard & Jane Wilson 2002. *The lighthouses of Trinity House.* Bradford on Avon: Thomas Reed Publications.

Wright, Frank Lloyd 1958. *The living city.* New York: Horizon Press.

Young, Robert W. & William Morgan Sr. (eds.) 1987 (revised edition). *The Navajo language: a grammar and colloquial dictionary.* Albuquerque: University of New Mexico Press.

Zukowksy, John (ed.) 1996. *Building for air travel: architecture and design for commercial aviation.* Chicago: Prestel/The Art Institute of Chicago.

Zukowksy, John (ed.) 2001. *2001: Building for space travel.* New York: Harry N. Abrams.

AGL Above Ground Level

AMD Active Mass Damper

AMSL Above Mean Sea Level

ARL Above Roof Level

BHAB British Helicopter Advisory Board

CBS Centraal Bureau voor de Statistiek (Statistics Netherlands)

CHUV Centre Hospitalier Universitaire Vaudois

HAGB Helicopter Association of Great Britain

HSAC Helicopter Safety Advisory Conference

IAATO International Association of Antarctica Tour Operators

ICAO International Civil Aviation Organization

IVW Inspectie Verkeer en Waterstaat (Transport and Water Management Inspectorate)

LPD Landing Platform Dock

MFB Monthly Film Bulletin

NAM Nederlandse Aardolie Maatschappij (Dutch Gas and Oil Company)

NYT New York Times

RAES Royal Aeronautical Society

REGA Rettungsflugwacht Garde Aérienne, Swiss Air Rescue

SAR Search and Rescue

Index

Helidrome Architecture

Helidrome Architecture

Helidrome Architecture

Acknowledgements

Instructors like Donald Kreuger, George Skala and their students and colleagues were my first sources of inspiration. The earliest explorations took place with Patricia Sabino on motorcycle, and with Monica Sabino by car. Their continuous support and the help of their friends has been the driving force of this work.

Assistance at libraries, archives and helipads was necessary and more than kind, and I need to mention Brian Riddle at the Royal Aeronautical Society, but also the librarians at the Los Angeles Public Library for their help. The generous support of the Geiger Family, Howard Cooper at Trinity House, Anjet Bastiaanse at the NAM and many others, such as Lisa Klikoff, Caroline Pack and Mickey Red who allowed or supplied photographs is much appreciated.

Then I need to thank all those who were willing to answer detailed questions about their language, city or country, and those who volunteered information of many kinds. Proof readers, university colleagues, friends and photographers such as Aart Mekking, Koos Bosma, John Zukowsky, Luuk Reurich, my father, and all those who have asked or were forced to see a glimpse of this manuscript, which was a Ph.D. thesis prior to being a book, have encouraged me to continue with this work until the end.

About the author

Alex de Voogt graduated from Leiden University as a linguist and received a Ph.D. in cognitive psychology from the same university in 1995. His main focus concerned the thinking processes of experts. The helicopter and its pilot also became part of his research interests when he started his training as a helicopter pilot in 1997. De Voogt obtained a commercial helicopter license in 2004, and he now works as an aviation psychologist at Maastricht University, the Netherlands.

Colophon

Text editing by George Hall
Photos by Alex de Voogt, unless otherwise stated
Graphic design by Piet Gerards Ontwerpers
(Piet Gerards & Janneke Vlaming)
Printed by Die Keure, Bruges

Cover photo by Alex de Voogt

© 2007 Alex de Voogt and 010 Publishers, Rotterdam
www.010publishers.nl

ISBN 978 90 6450 625 3